POLISHING THE DIAMOND,

ENLIGHTENING THE MIND

REFLECTIONS OF A

KOREAN BUDDHIST MASTER

POLISHING THE DIAMOND

◆

ENLIGHTENING THE MIND

Reflections of a
Korean Buddhist Master

Master Jae Woong Kim

Translated from the Korean
by Yoon Sang Han

WISDOM PUBLICATIONS • BOSTON

Wisdom Publications, Inc.
199 Elm Street
Somerville MA 02144 USA

Library of Congress Cataloging-in-Publication Data
Kim, Chae-ung, 1942–
    [Tangnŭn maŭm palgŭn maŭm. English]
    Polishing the diamond, enlightening the mind : reflections of
a Korean Buddhist master / Master Jae Woong Kim ; translated
from the Korean by Yoon Sang Han.
        p.   cm.
    Includes bibliographical references and index
    ISBN 0-86171-145-9 (pb : alk. paper)
    1. Religious life—Buddhism. I. Title.
BQ5410.K5318 1999   98-43093

                    ISBN 0-86171-145-9

                    04 03 02 01 00
                     6   5   4   3

                Design by: Gopa and the Bear
            Korean text on cover: *Mirŭk Chon Yŏrae Pul*

Wisdom Publications' books are printed on acid-free paper and meet
the guildelines for the permanence and durability of the Production
Guidelines for Book Longevity of the Council on Library Resources.

Printed in the United States of America.

For my incomparable teacher,

Master Baek Sung Wook.

Table of Contents

Foreword

Polishing the Diamond, Enlightening the Mind is a book compiled by Jae Woong Kim out of gratitude and devotion for his Korean Buddhist master, Baek Sung Wook. It contains the master's instructions and advice for cultivating the mind in the quest for enlightenment.

Despite wanting happiness and wishing to avoid suffering, human beings constantly engage in activities that give rise to fear, disease, starvation, and ultimately death. Under such circumstances it would be wonderful if even a few people could create some inner peace, if only for a short time. I am confident that readers who seek such a goal will find valuable advice in this book.

Venerable Tenzin Gyatso, the 14th Dalai Lama of Tibet
November 12, 1996

Publisher's Acknowledgment

THE PUBLISHER GRATEFULLY ACKNOWLEDGES the generous help of the Hershey Family Foundation in sponsoring the printing of this book.

Translator's Preface

THE KOREAN VERSION of *Polishing the Diamond, Enlightening the Mind* began originally as a collection of transcripts from Dharma lectures by Master Jae Woong Kim. In them, he conveyed the teachings of his teacher, Master Baek Sung Wook, who taught the essence of the Diamond Sutra. The Diamond Sutra is one of the most profound scriptures in Buddhism. Throughout history, Buddhist practitioners have believed that it contains the heart of Buddha's teachings. In *Polishing the Diamond, Enlightening the Mind*, Dharma Master Jae Woong Kim explains the teachings of the Diamond Sutra with examples and stories and shows how we can apply these teachings in our daily lives. Throughout the book, Master Kim stresses the practice of eradicating our karmic hindrances. Karmic hindrances are layers of self-created obstacles that we have accumulated over our many different incarnations, and they block us from becoming enlightened. It is important to stress that these root hindrances are accumulated within one's mind.

With the rising interest in Buddhism, various traditions have been introduced to the West. The Buddhist population in the West is steadily growing, yet Buddhism is still foreign to many Westerners. An American student in an introductory Buddhism class once asked, "When all is so empty, what is the point of living?" One of his classmates then replied, "It is the sound of one hand clapping." Although meant as a joke, such obscure interpretations of Buddhism can be found even among Buddhist practitioners, possibly reflecting a lack of practical understanding of how Buddhism relates to daily life.

Polishing the Diamond, Enlightening the Mind helps to clarify Buddhism and provides a simple Buddhist practice that anyone can do. Most importantly, this book shows us how Buddhism can be of benefit in our own lives. Master Kim transmits the teachings given to him by his own teacher, Master Baek Sung Wook, who was considered a living Buddha by many Koreans.

Traditionally, one had to forsake worldly life in order to be a serious Buddhist practitioner. Indeed, renouncing one's secular life was an essential part of the practice. In the beginning of *Polishing the Diamond, Enlightening the Mind*, however, Master Kim presents a simple Buddhist practice that he learned from Master Baek. Buddhist practices often include extensive sitting meditation. However, to retain the peacefulness of sitting meditation in the modern world, one has to be very advanced in meditation, and therefore such a practice is not practical for everyone. Master Kim's teacher found a practical method within the Diamond Sutra. When Master Kim first met his teacher, Master Baek told him, "Whenever a thought or an emotion occurs in your mind, offer it up to Buddha with reverence." This is the essence of the practice called *surrendering*. Using this method, Master Kim shows us how we can keep the peacefulness of sitting meditation in any situation. The rest of the book shows how we can enrich our lives by following the teachings of the Diamond Sutra. Throughout, Master Kim provides illustrations for his teachings, ranging from old tales to common problems that we encounter every day.

This book will be useful to anyone interested in Buddhism. Beginning practitioners will find *Polishing the Diamond, Enlightening the Mind* an easy introduction to the teachings of Buddha, while advanced practitioners will find it a guide to deepening their practice.

My special gratitude to His Holiness the 14th Dalai Lama for taking the time to read *Polishing the Diamond, Enlightening the Mind* and for his kind foreword to this book.

I would also like to thank the many people who have participated in the translation of *Polishing the Diamond*. I am especially grateful to my friends from Wesleyan University, Irene Kim, Terry Shanahan, Leah Sieck, and Jill Pfenning, who helped me with the translation from the beginning of this project. Also, much appreciation goes to my editor, Barbara Bergstrom, whose most challenging task, probably, was working with an ever-moving and mostly absent translator. My appreciation to all those others whom I have not named, whose help has made this translation possible. For their help, I am grateful, and I hold myself alone responsible for any errors or omissions.

—*Yoon Sang Han*

Introduction

The Enlightened Teacher,

Master Baek Sung Wook

———

STUDYING UNDER THE MASTER

THE FIRST TIME I met Master Baek was in April 1964. I was then twenty-four years old. Since my youth, I have believed that the fate of a nation rests on the education of its people. So, I thought that if we built a special teachers university and produced true teachers, we could better the character and conscience of all Koreans, eradicating our perpetual vices and bad habits. In order to set the foundation for this project, I started a small business. Also, to seek advice, I spent time meeting everyone who I thought was wise. It was through this project that I met Master Baek.

When Mr. Na Tong-yŏng, a graduate student of Dongguk University, told me that Master Baek was residing in the town of Sosa in Puch'ŏn City, in Kyŏnggi Province, I set out to find him. When I arrived there, I said that I came from Second Ŭlchi Avenue, Seoul, and that I wished to see Master Baek. Mr. Kim Ch'ŏl-su, who was attending the master at the time, led me to see him. Containing my excitement, I entered the quiet Buddha hall. Master Baek's presence was as blinding as the bright sunshine.

A hazy and luminous energy surrounded the area where Master Baek sat. With his solemn yet serene expression, he seemed to see straight through my mind. He had the look of an enlightened man who would not even allow a speck of karmic hindrance to remain in those who came before him. The moment I bowed down and sat in front of him, all my inner discriminations quietly settled down.

After a long silence, I stated the purpose of my visit and asked him if there was any way I could swiftly achieve my goal of building the special teachers university. He seemed to gaze at me for a long time when at last he told me that all I had to do was to follow his instructions. I was glad to hear this, so I quickly asked him, "What would you have me do, sir?"

He said, "I will tell you if you first say that you'll do it."

Since it is my nature to always honor my promises, I could not easily make this promise without some hesitation. A good while passed in silence.

"Will you do as I say or not?"

Silence.

Because there still was no answer from me, we sat quietly for a while. He then patiently asked me again, "Will you do as I say or not?"

Silence.

He asked me again. "Will you do it or not?"

Behind his three carefully and patiently repeated questions, there seemed to be a bright hope. I felt that the venture might be an auspicious one.

"Yes, I will do it, sir."

"Good. Read the Diamond Sutra both in the morning and in the evening and surrender any thought that arises in your mind to Buddha by reciting *Mirŭk Chon Yŏrae Pul* (Tathagata Maitreya—the future Buddha)."

Until then, I thought achieving social projects by reading sutras or by prayer was impossible, so I was very perplexed by his answer. But, as soon as I said, "Yes," my mind was illuminated as if white light had completely filled my heart. I felt a deep happiness. I felt like a lost ship struggling on a dark stormy ocean that had finally come upon a lighthouse. Only after a while did I realize the source of my happiness—meeting and studying under Master Baek has been my greatest *wŏn*, or vow, throughout this and many of my past lives.

After that first meeting, I visited Master Baek occasionally at Sosa to ask him questions. Later, I went to see him once a week, so that he could check my progress. Following his teachings, I put great effort into my practice. Even when I was busy running my business and living by myself, I read the sutra nine times a day. And as I gradually changed and expanded my business, I became single-mindedly determined to do a great work for society. During that time, my teacher seemed like such a kind, considerate person, checking every detail of my spiritual practice. His compassionate attention was like a warm spring breeze blowing through my heart, whisking away the dust of my bleak past.

In April 1966, after I had finished supporting my sister in her education, I entered the monastery at Sosa to study more seriously with Master Baek on his recommendation. But from the first day in the monastery, I felt as if I had been totally abandoned by my teacher. He was so strict and cold that I sometimes wondered why I went there in the first place.

Much later I came to understand that Master Baek's coldheartedness was actually his compassionate way of teaching. As a spiritual seeker who needed to devote all my mind and body to solving the problem of repeated birth and death, I needed to get rid of my dependence on him and develop a strong conviction of my own.

◆

Life at Sosa began at three in the morning, when we rose for our morning practice. At half past four, we listened to our master's Dharma lecture, and Master Baek would check the results of our previous day's practices. During these interviews, we revealed to our master all the intentions, realizations, dreams, and visions that had arisen in our minds, as if we were surrendering them to him. We then learned to cultivate our minds by working on the things that he pointed out.

Going to see my master the morning after a day when I had been unmindful made me feel like a cow being dragged to the slaughter house. Revealing my karmic hindrances in public was as painful as tearing out my own flesh, though this was the only way they would melt away and my mind would be cultivated.

My teacher used to say to us, "Release as many of your flaws as you can in front of me, and be the greatest person you can be outside of this place!" as he gently soothed every one of our karmic hindrances. During all those years, he never once missed checking our practice each morning. Much later, I began to see just how hard his task was.

My teacher perceived things beyond time and space. Two particular instances come to mind.

After seven and a half years of life at Sosa, I moved to P'ohang. There

I had breakfast at 10 A.M. and dinner at 2:30 P.M., but one day I was too busy to eat dinner on time. I became hungry later, so I ate some bread at 10 P.M. Back then, I used to go to Seoul once a month to visit my master to have my progress checked. When I went up to see him that time, he said to me, "I see that you couldn't even keep the schedule for your two meals a day, and instead you had to eat something around ten at night."

For the first eight months I was in P'ohang, I slept in a sitting position without reclining on anything. So, in the summertime, when I saw some people leaning against a tree to sleep in its shade, I felt envious. Then I even became tired of leaning against a wall during sleep and, a couple of days later, I started to sleep lying down. Soon thereafter I went to see my teacher, and somehow he knew that I had been sleeping on the floor, and he scolded me severely for not sleeping in a sitting position. He knew everything that was going on in P'ohang from three hundred miles away in Seoul. Probably nothing in this world is harder than attending a master who can see through your mind.

Once, when I was at Sosa, Master Baek had to go to Seoul. When he came back that night, he said he was sorry that he could not look after us when we needed him during the day. While living at the same place with us, he checked our mental state many times each day. He came to encourage the ones whose minds were faltering, and he always came to make a confirmation the moment Dharma awakened in one of us.

Among our daily tasks at Sosa Monastery, the first chore of the day was milking the cows, of which we had as many as fifteen at one point. The task of feeding, cleaning, and grazing the cows was itself overwhelming. On top of this, we did everything from cultivating fields to clearing waste lands. Our schedule was full of busy labor without rest.

One experience of milking the cows in the summer is still fresh in my memory. It was so hot and muggy that, even sitting still, I was bathed in sweat. Milking a cow on a day like that, with my right shoulder and face pressed against the cow's steamy leg and stomach, was unbearable. The worst times were when the cow would hit my mouth and eyes with her manure-caked tail as she tried to chase away the flies. What sickening moments those were! Nevertheless, I was truly grateful for the Dharma-hitting of the cow's tail, since the quick and intense surrender of my nauseating disgust helped me become awakened to so much wisdom. At those moments, the cow's tail was my teacher, enlightening my mind.

Once, I overheard my teacher mention to someone that the reason he had started a farm was to help spiritual seekers plant merit and to help their spiritual practice. While working on the farm and practicing our master's teaching, we came to realize that our labor and spiritual practice were not two different things. Also, while conditioning our consciousness to "work to feed others," we believed that everything we did, from eating to breathing, was a continuation of our efforts to serve the Buddha well.

Sentient beings' attachments to their bodies are embedded in sleeping, eating, and being comfortable. The practices we did, such as eating only two meals a day without any snack, continuously planting merit through hard work, and continuing to practice throughout the night, were all designed to stimulate our egos and our attachments to our bodies so that we could then surrender the attached states of mind that arose in such conditions. Karmic hindrances have to be cleansed from the mind the moment they arise; otherwise you lose your chance.

Cultivating my mind was as painful as carving out my bones. Our master's Dharma-hitting fiercely struck down on us every time we lost our mindfulness. The harsher the conditions, I suppose, the more pure and fragrant must the lotus flower blossom. This constant practice of surrendering my disdain for hard work, surrendering my attachments to eating and sleeping, surrendering the temptation to run away from the monastery, surrendering my karmic hindrances, and even surrendering the Buddha that I revered—all this made me truly understand, to the marrow of my bones, my teacher's goal when he first built the monastery: to raise Buddhas.

The place where I sacrificed life's most precious youth and all my destiny to serve Buddha, the place where I offered the highest reverence, the place where I devoted myself to my spiritual practice with the agony of crossing the line of life and death so many times a day—these memories of the monastery, along with my master's loving smile, have become part of the past that will never return. It is difficult for me to hide my sadness and longing, but I also surrender these feelings to the Buddha according to his teaching.

Cultivating your mind means curing your inner problems—wrong habits ingrained in you that give rise to wrongful acts. You cultivate the mind when you confront each crucial moment, each karmic hindrance, from your past lives. While I was trying so hard on my own to rid myself of bad habits, habits to which I had been conditioned over many past lives, my master helped me by hitting my karmic hindrances with his fist.

Once, my face turned bright red from his Dharma-hitting. And if it hurt someone as young as me so much, how painful it must have been for an old man like him, who at the time was close to eighty years old! Why was he going through so much trouble to teach an impossible person like me? I was so deeply moved by his compassion that I bowed down on the ground to him three times and cried my heart out.

FOLLOWING IN THE FOOTSTEPS
OF THE MASTER

MASTER BAEK WAS BORN on the nineteenth day of the eighth lunar month in the year 1897 in Seoul, Korea. He renounced the world —was ordained as a Buddhist monk—at the age of fourteen, graduated from Kyŏngsŏng Central Buddhist Institute when he was twenty-three, and went to Shanghai to participate in the Korean government-in-exile following the March 1st Korean Independence movement of 1919.

Later, he came to believe that, in order to achieve Korean liberation swiftly, Korean youth must have a modern education. Therefore, he set a goal to awaken, or educate, two hundred thousand young Koreans. In preparation for his project, he left Korea to study in Europe. After graduating from high school in Paris, he earned his Ph.D. in philosophy in 1925 from Wurzburg University in southern Germany with a dissertation entitled *Buddhist Metaphysics*, after which he returned to Korea.

He was a professor at the Central Buddhist Professional Institute for three years. However, because he was under strict surveillance by the Japanese police as a subversive character, and because the social conditions were not favorable at the time, he could not fulfill his earlier dream of educating two hundred thousand Korean youths. Prevented from achieving his goal, he retired from worldly life and entered the retreat at Kŭmgang Mountain in 1928. His reasons for entering the mountain retreat could only be for the liberation of Korea and for leading all beings to salvation.

A little while after he started his practice at the mountain, he became aware of the future of Korea and was assured of her liberation. He then thought about changing his body—passing on to the next life—because he had no more attachment to this world. However, looking further into the future, he saw that he still had tasks left at Sosa Monastery. Thus, he decided to continue his life.

He became enlightened while studying at Anyang-am and Chijang-am at Kŭmgang Mountain for ten years, and he taught many students at Chijang-am. In 1938, because of pressure from the Japanese police, he ended his practice among his students and returned home to practice alone in Seoul.

After Korean independence, Master Baek participated in establishing the Korean government. In 1950, he was inaugurated as Minister of Home Affairs and was active in setting the foundation of the country. Later he was in charge of the Public Corporation of Mining Promotion. With his wisdom-eye that could see sixteen feet underground, he found many tungsten deposits and thus gave some breathing room to the country's faltering economy.

In 1953, he became the president of Dongguk University, and during those hard social and economic times, he established the basis for today's Dongguk University. Furthermore, he pushed forward with many of his plans to make the university a world-class institution, though he did not get to see those plans come to fruition. Master Baek later commented on his attempt to raise Dongguk University's standard. He said that, since the people who were potentially at the receiving end of good fortune (the students of Dongguk University) lacked merit, even if someone wanted to provide them good fortune, the karma was not there for them to receive it.

In 1962, he retired from all of his social responsibilities and built a little monastery at the foot of Sosa's green hill. He became fully enlightened while residing there, and he immersed himself in enlightening the human nature of those with deep spiritual roots who came to see him. At the place where a carving of the Diamond Sutra passage "Thus ye shall view" hung instead of a doorplate, there remained the full radiance of my master's later years, along with the fierce efforts of other spiritual seekers.

According to his teaching "set your goal to Mahayana, but live your life as a Hinayana practitioner," Master Baek's daily life never deviated a bit from the proper life of a spiritual seeker. Since the time he entered the mountain retreat at the age of thirty-one, he always rose at the hour of the tiger (between 3 A.M. and 5 A.M.) to wash and begin his practice. He was so strict that he did not eat his meals if it were even five minutes past meal time, or "offering time," in the monastery.

Even while he was in public service, he never came out of his place of practice after 6 P.M. When he held the presidency at Dongguk University, he worked from early in the morning and came back to his place to practice in the afternoon after 3 o'clock.

Until he was over eighty years old, he always changed the briquette in his room and cleaned the ashes by himself, and he never let anyone do his laundry. Even when his students tried to attend to his chores, he always refused them and did them himself.

Master Baek devoted his entire life to serving Buddha and enlightening sentient beings. On the nineteenth day of the eighth lunar month in 1981, eighty-four years to the day after he was born, he entered *nirvana*, lying on his side, with a peaceful expression on his face.

ABOUT THE MASTER'S TEACHING

M ASTER BAEK ALWAYS TOLD US a few things during our morning interviews to help lead us to the path of enlightenment and to awaken us from our karmic hindrances. Following are a few quotes taken from these morning interviews.

Surrender to Buddha the thoughts, impressions, emotions, and ideas that arise in your mind. The practice of surrendering should be done out of the reverence that arises in your mind and not at someone else's request. If you do not surrender your thoughts out of reverence, you get caught up in dualistic thinking. You should surrender constantly. When surrendering is accompanied by reverence, you will attain bright wisdom, and you should put these realizations into practice. When you generate reverence to Buddha, there are no afterthoughts remaining, so there is no attachment to anything. You will realize and become aware of things as you constantly practice surrendering, but do not dwell on how you came to achieve those realizations. When reverence arises in you, you hear the Dharma lecture that completely fills the universe.

In cleansing one's attachment to sleep, do not say, "I am not sleeping." Instead say, "When do I have time to sleep, since I am full of reverence and joy?" The offering of the wŏn, or selfless vow, should be invoked naturally. But, if you say, "natural," you digress from the wŏn.

Surrender even the thought, "I have surrendered my arising thoughts again and again." If you think that you have surrendered many times, all you will have is the act of surrendering. The karmic hindrances you have accumulated for many eons will not leave you.

Master Baek always stressed that there should be a way to cultivate the mind that fits the lifestyle of modern people. Spiritual sects usually teach us to let go, cut, or calm our discriminating minds. But our master always said,

> When I do not have any power, with what strength can I cut the violent karma and sufferings that hide in and arise from the depth of my mind? If you say, "I" will let go of sufferings and delusions, you are only conditioning your ego. Therefore, surrender your sufferings and karmic retributions to Buddha with reverence.

Master Baek realized the practice of surrendering one's mind within the Diamond Sutra after starting his life at Sosa Monastery. Master Baek himself achieved full enlightenment through this method. He once commented on this method, saying,

> My level of enlightenment has been different at different periods in my life. My level at Kŭmgang Mountain was different, my level at Dongguk University was different, even my level at Sosa has been different from beginning, to middle, to end. You don't know how fortunate you all are. Do you know how tough a time I had before I realized this method of surrendering? Where else can you find people following such an easy path to enlightenment?
>
> When you offer up—surrender—your sufferings to Buddha, you accumulate merit through your offerings, you practice your reverence to Buddha, you free yourself from exchanging negative karma with others, and you can attain enlightenment. So, surrender your arising mind, thought, emotion, impression this very moment to Buddha with reverence.

Master Baek also said that the Diamond Sutra embodies the essence of Shakyamuni Buddha's spiritual attainment, for this Dharma lecture was given when his mind and body were the healthiest. If you compare it to the sun, his enlightenment was shining brilliantly like the sun at noon. This sutra is radiance itself. Therefore, Master Baek also said that if you read the sutra, which is Buddha's enlightenment and radiance, you face his wisdom. By becoming one with his radiance, you free yourself from the shadow of karmic hindrance and misfortune and enlighten your human nature.

The practices he recommended, including the method of surrendering, are:

> While reciting *Mirŭk Chon Yŏrae Pul* with your mind, hear it through your ears, and practice surrendering all your thoughts to the Buddha. If you hold on to the thoughts in your mind, they will cause you to become ill. If you suppress them, they will explode. Surrendering is the spiritual seeker's "conquest of mind." Read the Diamond Sutra in the morning and in the evening. Learn it as if you are actually in front of the Buddha, learning directly from him, and make a habit of practicing what you have learned. Let your body work regularly, but keep your mind absolutely still.
>
> If you do this for one hundred days and repeat the hundred-day practice about ten times, you will attain the ability to see your past lives and to see others' past lives as well, because your ego will have melted away. This could be called the attainment of beginning Buddhist practice.
>
> You should be cautious of saying, "I am going to devote myself to practice," for that is the mind of greed. If you say, "my practice is going well," that is the mind of ignorant arrogance. And if you say, "my practice isn't going well," that is the mind of anger. Therefore, not doing those three is the practice of the path. Practice diligently, and as long as you do not *not do* your practice, you will be fine.
>
> An ancient sage said, "Practice unceasingly, not intensely."

I suppose anyone would become nostalgic at the thought of an unforgettable teacher, but my recollection of the enlightened Master Baek Sung Wook and the times when I studied under him at Sosa is particularly special. I think with fondness of those days when I cleansed myself of karmic hindrances and served Buddha with only his teachings as my guide. I am grateful for his teachings, and if he were here, I would tell him this:

> Because you scolded me severely at times to eradicate my karmic hindrances, and because at other times you kindly soothed me to strengthen my faltering mind, I am at least able to serve Buddha this much. To me, who had been lost and wandering like an orphan in endless time and in an infinite universe, you gave a bright lamp.
>
> Even now, ten years since you entered nirvana, you are still alive and clear in my mind. I see you in my practice, and whenever I have a question, your face appears first in my mind. I even surrender this mind that reveres you. I cannot describe the sense of loss I feel, not having you to bow to with all my heart.
>
> Now that I have matured a little, I am so grateful for the things that you have done for me that sometimes I can hardly stop my tears. I know that to serve your teachings is to enlighten my own mind and to spread your method for cultivating the mind. Also, in order to prepare a seat for you when you return, I invoke a wŏn to Buddha with all my heart. May this wŏn come true to serve Buddha well and to plant much merit.
>
> *Polishing the Diamond, Enlightening the Mind* has been published with the intention of serving Buddha and of serving you. Along with Dharma lectures that I received from you, I have added some of my own thoughts. This book is the compilation of what I have said during Dharma meetings to people who are following the path. I am worried that I might not have correctly conveyed your profound realm; but, despite my worries and the

limitations of this book, I carefully offer it up to you, my teacher, to the Buddha, and to the numerous Buddhas of the future.

One

The World That Is Created

by the Mind

SOUND OF A BELL

ONCE, WHEN KANG XI, the second emperor of the Qing Dynasty, was a crown prince he went to Wu Tai Mountain to meditate. He usually practiced Chan (Zen). One day, as he was taking a walk around the temple grounds, he heard an evening bell toll. Suddenly, the ringing no longer came from the bell, but it peacefully resonated from deep within his mind.

Upon experiencing such a rare phenomenon, he asked one of the courtiers by his side with great delight, "How does that bell sound to you?" A monk standing next to the courtier, who was not even addressed by the prince, abruptly interrupted the conversation to impress the prince, saying, "My lord, even the sound of a black crow is Buddha's teaching." In that moment, a severe disgust arose in the prince's mind at the way the monk tried to impress him, completely destroying the prince's *samadhi*—the meditative state characterized by calm, stability, and the absence of distraction.

According to Master Baek, hearing the sound of the bell as the sound of one's mind is a hard level to achieve for a spiritual practitioner because it means that one's ego has melted away. He said that if the ringing resembles the sound of the bell and the sound of your mind, your practice is halfway there. If the ringing sounds like it comes entirely from the bell, then you should know that you are just starting on your spiritual path. To test our stages of development, our teacher asked us from time to time where we thought the sounds from outside—such as that of a bell, gong, or carriage—were coming from.

THE IMAGE IN THE MIND

I N THE PAINTINGS of Kim Ŭn-ho, the images of Sin Saimdang (an ideal Korean mother and wife) and Nongae (a patriotic heroine) look similar. Although the appearances of Sin Saimdang and Nongae should be different, the reason that they give out such similar feelings is because there is only one image of a woman that the artist reveres. Even among the portraits of women by many Western artists, we see that each artist does not stray far from a single feeling. This is because there is only one image of a beautiful woman in the mind of every artist.

Just as there are images of ideal women in the minds of artists, when we say we worship God or Buddha, wouldn't our God or Buddha be none other than our mind's image of God or Buddha? Since my image of Buddha is different from everyone else's, such a Buddha is probably only my own idea.

Most of us revere and live with a God or Buddha who is limited by our own imagination and experiences. Isn't this true "idol worship"? To surrender my idea, the idol, is true spiritual practice. When you can surrender your ideas, which are shadows in your mind, only then will you truly perceive Buddha.

Even with religion, Buddha, or the truth—if you enclose them in your mind, they become nonreligion, an idol, and a nontruth. If your mind is covered by the shadows of "truth" or "religion," your wisdom is tarnished before you even begin. There is a saying that goes, "Do not stay where Buddha is and run away from where there is no Buddha." Surrendering each arising thought is truly the noble thing to do.

A MILLIONAIRE'S KARMIC RETRIBUTION

ONCE, THERE WAS a wealthy American industrialist who, as he was accumulating his wealth, ate less in order to hoard money. Even after he became a tycoon, he cared so much about his money that once, when a public phone did not return his coin, he went all the way to the phone company to get his money back. He changed his mind just before he was about to sign his name on a complaint card.

His stingy habits of not eating and not spending were so severe that eventually his mind became hardened. In his later years, he could no longer eat. He tried all sorts of methods, but still he could not eat. Finally, he announced that he would share a large portion of his wealth with anyone who could feed him for a week.

Then, a doctor came up with a brilliant idea. He told the man to invite one hundred babies to a huge dinner party and to serve those babies himself. The babies, as usual, spilled and dropped their food as they ate. The man couldn't stand to see the food being wasted, so he hastily picked it up and ate it. Since he opened his mind to feed other people, he accumulated merit, and, through his merit, his hungry ghost karma was momentarily calmed.

In order for the millionaire to cure his disease completely, he needed to purify his mentality of eating less to save money, a habit he had been practicing for a long time. If, at seventy years old, he had been practicing this stingy mind since he was twenty, then he would have had fifty years' worth of poison to surrender to the Buddha.

When you begin spiritual practice, you regress to your past to purify your mind. Cultivating your mind today will free yesterday's and the day before yesterday's mind. Continuing one more day will cleanse your mind from three days and four days ago. Cultivating your mind for three days will purify your mind from six days ago, seven days ago, and so on.

If the American industrialist had regressed back twenty years by practicing in this way, he could have completely cured his illness. It would have been similar to when subconscious problems are cured in psychotherapy. Cultivating one's mind means surrendering not only the diseased aspect of the mind that has been accumulating in one's subconscious, but also surrendering *every* conditioned human discrimination, leaving no trace, neither good nor bad.

REGARDLESS OF WHO YOU ARE, if you harbor hatred against others, you will be hated by others, because the being who is closest to your hateful mind is you, your own body and no one else's.

If you respect others, due to your respectful mind you will be respected by others. Looking down on others and trying to be above everyone else will instead put you below everyone else. Thus it is said that if you look down on others, you will be short of stature in your next life. Since the mind that is belittling others is your own, you yourself will appear stunted. One who views others as undesirable will have an undesirable face, while one who respects and looks up to others will have a noble and handsome appearance.

If a human hits an animal such as a cow or a dog, he imprints the animal's image strongly in his own mind because of his hate. He could easily be reborn as that kind of animal in his next life. And, since the animal imprints the abusive human in its mind, if it goes on to receive a human body, it is likely to become an abusive person. This is a stern reality of the law of the mind.

If you have to catch roaches, ants, or flies, catch them not with the mentality of killing them, but with the intention of cleaning your environment. If your intention is to clean your environment, in this case the environment where you practice—the Buddha-hall, you will imprint this cleansing of defilements on the Buddha-hall. However, if you catch insects with the intention of killing them, you imprint killing in your mind.

Also, if you are forced into a war, you have to face the war with the intention of sweeping away the enemy forces in order to defend your nation and your people, not with the intention of shooting down every enemy soldier. If you were to have the mentality of killing each one, a vendetta between you and the dead ones would begin. Whereas if you have the intention of clearing away the entire enemy, it becomes merely a contest between one group and another.

Among the emperors of the Qing Dynasty, six were enlightened. Emperor Kang Xi ruled without killing anyone. The others, when forced into wars, used this expression of clearing the enemy force.

A general, Paek Kae, became insane, however, because of guilt he felt for murdering ten thousand soldiers who had surrendered to him. Also, Cao Cao, in his last moment, was frightened to death by haunting images of all the people who were wrongfully killed due to his mistakes. He died in horror. As Cao Cao's mind weakened, all the regrets imprinted in his mind arose to terrify him.

We plant merit with our minds, and we commit crimes with our minds. With our minds, we imprint images. This one mind is like an artist. It can draw anything, and what it draws is realized. If you surrender your impressions, ideas, thoughts, and so on at the moment they arise without imprinting them on your mind, your mind will not be tainted, just as the lotus flower is not tainted by the muddy water from whence it grows.

SURRENDER EVEN THE SINS

IN LORD BUDDHA'S TIME, two monks were meditating diligently in a cave on the mountain. One day, the sister of one of the monks brought their daily supplies to the cave, but her brother was not around. Only his friend was there. Out of some strange karmic connection, she and her brother's friend made love. As a result, the monk had to face the tragedy of being banished from the order.

The girl's brother later came back to the cave and heard the story from his sad and distressed friend, a spiritual seeker who had committed an irreversible sin and whose hope of enlightenment was over. He could only agonize in deep despair. After the other monk heard the story, he accused his own sister of crushing his friend's eternity. He put all the blame upon her for his friend's banishment, and he killed her.

Enlightenment, which he felt was more important than his sister's life, might just have been in his eyes a sole wish, or a bitter grudge, that all spiritual seekers carry. Perhaps they consider enlightenment more important than life itself, and their struggle to become enlightened for many lifetimes is almost a vengeance.

One, banished, and the other, a murderer, together they went to see Venerable Upali. Clinging to a last strand of hope, they told him what had happened and asked Venerable Upali if people like them could still be saved. Venerable Upali bluntly said that salvation was impossible for them even if they were to repent.

The two monks lost all hope and began lamenting. Just then, Vimala-kirti, who was passing by, saw them with his wisdom-eye. He realized that their good roots had in fact been planted deeper than those of Venerable Upali. He had to save their dead minds, so he began a Dharma lecture to the three of them.

Venerable Upali, you should not make their sins any heavier. You have to end their worries and remorse so that their minds will not shake any more. The true nature of sin is neither within, without, nor in between.

As the Lord Buddha has said, "If the mind is impure, the sentient being is impure, and if the mind is pure, the sentient being is pure."

Mind is neither within, without, nor in between. And since the mind is this way, so is the sin. Likewise, everything else is the same way: nothing cannot exist beyond its true nature.

Venerable Upali, when the mind has attained enlightenment, does the mind have any defilement? No, it does not. Likewise, delusions are pure if there is no impurity. If there is no wrong thought, the mind is pure. Being attached to the self is defilement, and not being attached to the self is purity. Like the haze, the moon's reflection on water, and an image reflected on a mirror, all conditioned things are created by delusion. Only the one who knows this is enlightened.

At that moment, a bright ray of hope shone into their dark and hopeless hearts, and the two monks were able to awaken the pure *bodhi* mind once more.

SCOLDING TAINTS THE MIND

L ONG AGO, many bandits roamed the mountains, and they often captured monks. It was said that, less than three years after their capture,
the monks began to commit the same crimes, crimes to which they once
had been vehemently opposed.

During those three years, every time the captured monks called the
bandits "cruel robbers" and "horrible murderers" and watched their acts
in horror, the monks photographed those images in their minds. Eventually, those images became their minds. It is very hard to control a mind
that has become hardened due to imprinting images of harsh scolding
based on conscience and morality.

There are many such examples of people becoming what they criticize,
after scolding other people's actions with their minds. The child who
became a stutterer after teasing another stuttering child, the daughter-
in-law who criticized her mother-in-law and became worse than her
mother-in-law, and so on. They all learn while they scold. Every time
you see someone else's fault, you should know that such criticizing is
your own mind and be able to surrender that mind.

The mind is like a film. If you develop what you have photographed
in your mind, it becomes your life. What you imprint on your mind
gets played like a movie on a screen called the universe. You yourself
become a true actor. When, however, you surrender all the images in
your mind, your weary journey also ends.

Two

Surrendering the Mind

to Buddha

JOY AT SEEING
YOUR KARMIC HINDRANCES

ONCE, a certain *posallim*, or female Buddhist practitioner, went to the New Year's Day prayer gathering at the Temple of the Seven Buddhas. Despite the cold weather, many practitioners were prostrating or reciting Buddha's name all night in front of a stone Buddha that stood in the middle of the temple grounds.

Since the posallim was wearing many layers of clothing, she felt uncomfortable in her wool coat. She took off her coat and hung it in a room, then bowed and prayed in front of the stone Buddha until dawn. By that time it had gotten colder, so she went back to the room to get her coat so that she might continue praying.

The room had been heated all night by a large fire, and it was so hot that some of the floor mats were slightly burnt. A couple of posallims were sleeping on the floor instead of praying all night. The scene did not please her. She looked everywhere for her coat and finally found someone sleeping on top of it so as to lessen the heat from the floor. Filled with rage, she examined the coat and found that it was all wrinkled, with some spots even slightly burnt.

She was about to wake the woman who was sleeping on top of the coat and yell at her, but she restrained herself, thinking, "Since the coat is already in this condition, yelling at her will not iron out the wrinkles or repair the burns." She also rationalized that, on her way up to the temple, she could have ripped the coat by getting it stuck on a branch, or lost it entirely, so she convinced herself it was a good thing that only this much damage had occurred.

After her trip, the posallim came to me and asked me if showing such restraint is how the practice of surrendering is done. Surrendering, however, does not mean restraining or rationalizing one's emotion like that. The moment she thought it was not proper for those women to sleep on the floor, the scolding mind of anger had already surfaced in her mind. The person who practices surrendering well without losing mindfulness would have started to surrender his or her criticism at that very moment. If she had surrendered well at that moment, she probably would not have been so angry when she first found someone sleeping on her coat. If she were not able to do that, she could have at least surrendered her anger the moment she was overwhelmed with rage, even though it was a little late. Instead, she let her anger escape. Surrendering does not mean going through a process of restraining or rationalizing one's emotion, but rather surrendering that emotion directly by reciting Buddha Maitreya's name, *Mirŭk Chon Yŏrae Pul.*

The instant anger arises in you, you should cleanse it from your mind and be free of it immediately. You should surrender your anger until there is no remnant of it left in you. Also, you should practice surrendering in such a way that the time it takes to cleanse the discriminative notion from your mind gradually diminishes.

Hardened karmic hindrances accumulated in your mind can be surrendered only if they are first revealed through external shocks, just as we remove the dirt in the bottom of a well by stirring its water with a long stick and collecting the surfacing sediments. There is a saying that goes, "Liberation is being happy to see your karmic hindrances arise." This shows us the attitude of a spiritual seeker: always ready.

NOT HOLDING ONTO DELUSIONS

ONCE I HAD TO VISIT a senior acquaintance of mine, so I bought some strawberries at the marketplace before I went over to his home. An elderly lady of the household washed the strawberries with just a little water from a small kettle and put them out in a bowl to serve to the guests. I thought the strawberries should have been washed many times with more water to clean off the dirt, bugs, and pesticides. When I saw her washing them with only one bowl of water, I did not think the berries would be clean enough.

Because I am very particular about cleanliness, Master Baek once called me a person "who would even wash water before drinking it." There was no way I would eat those strawberries.

How uncomfortable it is to have the notion of uncleanliness in one's mind! Even though I did not touch the strawberries, I imprinted dirty strawberries in my mind, which will cause me later to pick and eat only dirty fruit. And if I had eaten those strawberries, my uncomfortable feeling would probably have continued, and I might have had to vomit. Or, since I would have felt that bacteria were running around in my stomach, I might have had to go to a hospital right away to feel better.

All these notions are one mind's working. Whether one actually eats the strawberries or not, surrendering a single notion of uncleanliness without keeping it in one's mind, until that notion disappears from one's mind, is the true practice of surrendering. If you surrender the notion of uncleanliness, you could either eat or not eat the strawberries depending on the situation, but there is no discomfort from your "notion of uncleanliness." Thus, you would remain calm. A calm and indifferent mind is evidence that you have surrendered the discriminating mind.

SURRENDERING
WHILE WATCHING THE MIND

THE PRACTICE of constantly watching one's mind is the basis of spiritual practice. If you did not look to other people or objects but always looked into your mind, your mind would not leave you to follow the people you meet on the streets. When your mind is always with the reverence of surrendering, you are being mindful.

Since you do not know when basic karmic hindrances such as laziness, hatred, or lust will arise from your inner world, absentmindedness should be avoided as much as walking on thin ice. Being absentminded means you are not watching your mind carefully.

Timing is very important in the practice of surrendering. A violent karmic hindrance is especially difficult to surrender after it has already surfaced. While constantly watching your mind, you should start surrendering the moment a hindrance tries to take its position and surface in your mind. By the time it plants its roots and spreads its branches, it is very hard to surrender.

Once, a posallim had an automobile accident. After the accident, she became frightened of cars at the mere sight of one. When she had to walk in the streets, she was in constant fear, and if she had to ride in a car, she would hide her face behind newspapers. This continued even six months after the accident.

I recommended that she read the Diamond Sutra and also intensely surrender her fears and the memory of the accident whenever they arose in her mind. I asked her to surrender with strong determination, so as not to lose her mindfulness even for a moment—especially if she had to ride in a car. After she had tried it for fifteen days, she became totally liberated from the fears that she had imprinted in her mind, and seeing cars did not bother her anymore.

This posallim freed herself in fifteen days from fears that she had imprinted in her storehouse consciousness for six months. If she had been proficient in surrendering daily at the time of the accident, she would have been able to surrender her rising fearful intuition the moment the accident occurred, or right before it happened. If she had been able to completely surrender at that moment, in that split second, she might have been able to free herself from the karmic causes that resulted in the accident, thus avoiding the accident altogether. Even if that were not the case, her karmic retribution would have diminished, and she could have lessened the damage of the accident. Also, since her fears would have decreased in accord with her surrendering, she would have experienced less mental trauma. Even after the accident, if she had surrendered her shock as soon as possible, her suffering would not have lasted for six months.

It may safely be said that we are devoting ourselves to spiritual practice in order to use it just once—at the critical moment of our death. Therefore, in order not to forget your practice at shocking moments, you should always practice watching your mind without losing mindfulness.

The Buddha once asked one of his students, "What is the span of human life ?"

The student answered, "It is a couple of days, Lord."

The Buddha said, "You do not know the practice yet."

The Buddha asked another student, "What is the span of human life?"

The student answered, "It is the time between meals, Lord."

The Buddha replied, "You also do not know the practice yet."

Again, he asked a different student, "What is the span of human life?"

The student answered, "It is the time between inhaling and exhaling, Lord."

The Buddha said, "You indeed know the practice."

Spiritual practice lies in not losing our mindfulness even in such a short moment as the time between breaths. Thus we should practice surrendering moment after moment.

SURRENDERING THE MIND TO BUDDHA

IF YOU HOLD ON to the endless thoughts and inner discriminations arising in your mind, they will cause illness. If you suppress them, they will explode. But if you surrender those delusions to Buddha, then the mind that has been emptied will be completely filled with Buddha's radiance.

Swiftly surrender arising discriminative notions to Buddha

If there were all sorts of sediments—such as pieces of paper, rice, leaves—in the bottom of a large, deep well, what would you do to clean it? If the well had too much water and if the water kept flowing in, so that you could not pump out the water from the well, you would have to stir the water with a paddle. As the water swirled, all the sediments would rise to the surface. Then, you could clean the well by simply sitting on the side and collecting the surfacing waste with a bowl.

Our minds are like the well. There are many karmic hindrances that have settled in the bottom of our minds here and there. If we were mindful in our everyday lives and immediately surrendered to Buddha the karmic hindrances rising from the bottom of our minds, our minds would be cleansed. The paddle that stirs the well is like the shocks from outside that stir our minds. The waste that rises is like our karmic hindrances that we have to surrender, and collecting the dirt with a bowl is like the practice of surrendering.

When you continue to surrender, you surrender the notion of "everyday life," the notion of "not losing the mindfulness," the notion of "discriminating minds," and you even surrender the notion of "surrendering to Buddha." Furthermore, even the afterthoughts of those thoughts are surrendered.

All arising inner discriminations are only my mind

When we are scolded by someone, anger erupts in our minds, and we decide the one who scolded us is a terrible person. But if the same person praises us, joy—that has been dwelling in our minds—arises to praise him or her as a nice person.

Whether I think the other person is nice or terrible, it is only an opinion in my mind, and this opinion has nothing to do with the other person. Instead of looking into our own minds, we usually project our discriminating minds onto others and quarrel with them. If there is no hatred in me, I will not hate others, and if there is no anger in me, I will not be angry with others. If the hatred in my mind is extreme, a person who bothers me will be hated to the extent that there is hatred in me.

Like ice melts away under the sun, karmic hindrances
melt away under the radiance of the Buddha

When anger arises, intensely surrender it by reciting *Mirŭk Chon Yŏrae Pul* to that emotion. Your karmic hindrance will melt away little by little each time you recite Buddha's name, just as ice melts away in the sunshine.

Anger arises because of external disturbances, and soon it subsides back into your mind again. If you intensely surrender the anger before it settles back, it will melt away just as much as you have surrendered.

Even if you were able to surrender your anger only so much, the rage that seemed to suffocate you would disappear, and it would bother you only a little. If you surrender it over and over, so that there is no anger left in you, then even if you were humiliated by others, you would simply be calm since there would be no anger in you. You might even be able to give them a peaceful smile.

This is an enlightened person's level. Whether it is the angry mind, sad mind, despising mind, or greedy mind, if you surrender it, you can be freed from it. With *Mirŭk Chon Yŏrae Pul*'s white radiance, there is no karmic hindrance from which we cannot free ourselves. Even if one of your karmic hindrances were as thick as the earth itself, if you did not miss your chance to intensely surrender it, it could be melted away.

Making offerings with one's mind is what makes Buddha happy

Some people say that presenting nice flowers or fruits to Buddha is the true offering. They argue that surrendering karmic hindrances—such as our suffering minds or hatred—to Buddha cannot be considered a true offering. The reason Buddha came to this world, however, was to enlighten all sentient beings. Therefore, offering up one's discriminations, thereby getting closer and closer to enlightenment, is the service that will make him the happiest. The merit of making a saint happy is the merit that lights up the entire universe.

When you surrender your repulsive karmic hindrances, one by one, 84,000 discriminative notions become one less: 83,999. If you are freed from one discrimination, one bright light takes the vacated place in your mind; if you surrender two discriminative notions, two lights will take their place. Eventually, when you surrender all 84,000 discriminating minds, bright light fills up all the emptied places in your mind and lights up the entire universe.

When your mind is deeply tranquil, when the brightness of your mind is complete within and without, your mind will know all things without a shred of doubt. This brightness or radiance can mean the nondual wisdom that perceives the true nature of things, rather than actual light or luminosity. That state of powerful energy and joyous white radiance is a state that defies human description. Only with reverence may we serve Buddha well—*parwŏn*, I offer this wŏn!

ANALOGY FROM
THE AVALOKITESHVARA SUTRA

Tang dynasty's Han Yu once went to see Zen Master Tai Dian and asked him, "According to the Avalokiteshvara Sutra, if a storm and tidal waves are about to overturn a ship and send everyone on it to a land of demons, and even one person among the panic-stricken crowd were to recite *Namu Kwanseйm Posal* (Bodhisattva Avalokiteshvara), the water would be calmed and the disaster avoided. Why is that?"

Zen Master Tai Dian answered, "I heard some bitch got laid and bore a son of a bitch. Is that your mother?"

To a powerful man of the Tang Dynasty, this was an outrageous insult. Han Yu wanted to pull out his sword and strike down the master at once, but since he had been embarrassed by the master before, he suppressed his humiliation instead and left the place. He later told the story to a student of Master Tai Dian, and the student said, "How much better could the master have lectured you on that? That was an excellent lesson."

Dumbfounded, Han Yu questioned him further. The monk went on, "In sutras, there are many analogies to cultivating one's mind. The Avalokiteshvara Sutra is the same way. The heart of that analogy is to purify the anger, which destroys one's surroundings, from the mind by reciting Avalokiteshvara Bodhisattva's name.

"When you hurt others and quarrel with others because of your anger, it is like being in the same danger as the boat with many people that is about to be shipwrecked in a storm. When you surrender the anger by reciting Avalokiteshvara's name, your mind will become peaceful, as if the storm and tidal waves had stopped, and your surroundings will also be at peace.

Because the master is full of compassion, he gave you an excellent lecture. He wanted you to actually experience his answer, despite the anger it would evoke in you."

After listening to the monk's explanation, Han Yu said to him, "Your explanation has awakened me even more than the master's sermon," and he thanked the monk.

Since the old days, it is said that "anger is the fire in one's mind that burns away all of one's virtuous deeds." Anger should be absolutely surrendered by reciting Buddha's name.

THREE POISONS:
GREED, HATRED, AND IGNORANCE

Greed

B ECAUSE A HUMAN BEING has a body, he needs a house to live in, food
to eat, and clothes to wear. However, even if our physical needs are
taken care of, we still crave with our mind. This craving mind is called
t'amsim. If you try to eradicate greed from your mind, you will feel
impoverished. Therefore, you should realize what you truly need and
take care of these needs. You should also realize the amount of merit
that has been previously planted in your mind.

There are two types of greed: the craving that wants to possess material goods, called *kant'amsim*, and the craving that wants to possess a
person, which we see in relationships between men and women, called
ŭmt'amsim.

When you cling to things—whether physical or spiritual—you condition yourself to have a long body like that of a snake in your next life.
Because you are trying to grasp much with a small body, your body will
become longer. Before you cling to things such as a higher position,
before you crave it, invoke a wŏn to Buddha, wishing that everyone else
would ascend to a higher position.

Even enlightenment becomes problematic if you cling to it. If you
devote yourself to the spiritual practice in order to serve Buddha, you
will be enlightened easily. But if you say, "I am going to get enlightened," then enlightenment becomes very difficult. Such an intention is
greed, therefore, you should surrender that greed—that ardent desire to
become enlightened—to Buddha and learn to truly follow the path of
enlightenment.

Greed is an unhealthy mind and the source of misfortune. It should
be purified both by realizing one's true needs and by practicing

charity toward others without expecting any reward. Look at the mind of one who has not eaten for a day, or the mind of one who has lost his or her loved one to someone else. Such a desperate mind is the mind of a wild beast. Such wild emotions should be surrendered intensely to Buddha in order to liberate them from your mind.

After getting rid of your greed, confronting others' greed is like putting a cow made of clay into water. Once you get rid of the karmic hindrance in your own mind, others' karmic hindrances will melt away too.

Anger (hatred)

Just as ashes are the only remains of fire, destruction is the only remnant of the path of anger. Anger brings poison to the mind and fiery karmic retribution to the body. An angry mind is an unhealthy mind. It is a source of misfortune and disaster. An angry mind is like a fire—it dries our blood and burns our flesh. Whether it is heartstricken vengeance, intense hatred, or fright and anxiety, there is no discriminating mind that cannot be purified by the white radiance of *Mirŭk Chon Yŏrae Pul.* When an ironlike, suffocating, karmic hindrance arises in you, if you surrender that to Buddha, it pleasantly melts away like ice melting under the sun, and your mind calms down, attaining wisdom.

At first it might take thirty minutes or an hour to surrender your anger. Later, it could be shortened to just five minutes or even one minute. After a while, you will be able to surrender your anger by reciting *Mirŭk Chon Yŏrae Pul* just once. Sometimes, right before the anger arises, the very moment it begins to form in you, you might be able to surrender your anger just by calling out the first character, *"Mi."*

Always look into your mind. The reaction that arises from others' praise is your mind, and the reaction that arises from others' scolding is also your mind. Therefore, do not look outside of your mind, but look inside it and completely surrender the arising thoughts and emotions. After getting rid of your anger, confronting others' anger is, once again, like putting a cow made of clay into water.

Ignorance

If you desire to be treated well and to be served by others, you are only practicing attachment to your body. If you are not willing to learn from the world, your wisdom cannot grow. You will be separated from the wisdom of the universe, and yours will be a life of complete darkness.

If you practice the ignorant (arrogant) mind, you start to dislike everyone. An ignorant mind is an unhealthy mind, and it is a source of disaster, misfortune, and no wisdom. It presents darkness to the mind and sufferings to the body. An ignorant person treats himself like his own enemy.

Instead, see everyone as a Buddha. You will discover many of Buddha's actions from these numerous future Buddhas, and you will be able to learn from them. Thus, through these Buddhas' scoldings and punishments, it will be hard not to examine yourself and hard not to be awakened by them.

King Yu of China bowed to anyone who pointed out his faults. He thanked them very deeply, because without their insight he would have had to live with the heavy burden of his limitations. One of Confucius's students said to Confucius, "Look over there: a thief is being taken away by a policeman." Confucius then said, "I guess your teacher is passing by." The student then asked Confucius, "Why is he my teacher?" Confucius replied, "Isn't that thief ruining his life to teach you and everyone else a great lesson—to show us the results of crime? When we know that the events of the world are our lessons and teachers, we further our drive for learning. Our realizations will illuminate our wisdom."

If you think your practice has progressed much, remember that such a belief comes only from your mind—it is neither the result of invoking a wŏn to Buddha nor of not invoking a wŏn. Surrender your belief that your practice has progressed much, as well as the belief that your practice has not progressed much. If you cling to the notion that you have been practicing for a long time, you have only that notion in your mind, and there is no place for Buddha. Therefore, awaken your conviction again and again. Renounce the world, renew your determination, over and over, and surrender even the notion that you have surrendered.

MIND'S POISON AND BODY'S DISEASE

IN MANY CASES, the actions of our minds control our diseases. If a cow drinks water it becomes milk, but if a snake drinks water it becomes poison. Depending on how we use our minds, the results of our diseases are infinitely varied.

The poison generated by one's mind comes out mostly in the form of greed or anger. If the poison spreads through greed, it causes diseases, such as stomach cancer, ulcer, or gastritis, in one's digestive organs. If the poison spreads through anger, it causes diseases in one's respiratory organs, such as the lungs or bronchial tubes.

Swelling in your head or swelling that sprouts out on the back of your neck, on your thigh, or on your legs is caused by the poison generated in your mind spreading to your body. Even fatigue can be seen as being caused by the poison in your mind together with your body's exhaustion. If you spew out the mind's poison through your mouth, it becomes negative karma of the mouth. Someone who accumulated much negative karma of the mouth in his past life, or who spewed out many poisonous words, has faulty teeth.

Sometimes the mind's poison can spread directly to the environment. Just as in the Korean saying, "A woman's slander can bring frost in May and June," one person's poisonous mind can torment the people around him. If a manager of a company has a bad day at home and vents his anger on his section chief, the section chief would then vent his anger on his foreman, and the foreman would vent his anger on hundreds of factory workers. The poison would then spread like the ripples formed by a rock thrown into a pond. Thus, the health of the mind is directly related to the health of the body and to the health of society.

May we thoroughly surrender the three poisons, so that we can serve Buddha well, parwŏn!

CHARITY *(poshi)*. Treat others with the mind of giving, and practice doing works that have no reward. The perfection of *poshi* purifies the mind of greed.

Ethical restraint *(chigye)*. Do not dwell on regrets. Try to lessen the regrettable incidents in your life. The perfection of *chigye* purifies the mind of anger.

Patient endurance *(inyok)*. See everyone as a Buddha. It is for you to realize and learn the Buddha's perfection of *inyok*. The perfection of *inyok* purifies the mind of ignorance and arrogance.

Zealous effort *(chŏngjin)*. The first three perfections are the laws that you should apply to the world as a human being. If they are right, then practice them with diligence. This is the perfection of *chŏngjin*.

Stability of mind *(sŏnjŏng)*. Through the practices above, as time passes, your mind will become calm. This is the perfection of *sŏnjŏng*.

Wisdom *(panya)*. When you are used to these perfections, your mind will become peaceful and attain wisdom. Thus, you will have no doubts in your actions. This is the perfection of *panya*.

—*from a Dharma lecture by Master Baek*

Three

Purifying the Mind

Enlightening the Mind

———

SURRENDERING THE HATRED

ONE HUMAN BEING hating another is a great tragedy. But, since we are human, we live with hatred in our minds. Buddha called this hatred suffering. The exchange of hatred between family members or between colleagues at work, for example, is the suffering of having to live with someone you consider your enemy.

However, one who serves Buddha surrenders his or her hatred to Buddha instead of blaming others. When you dislike someone, do not look to that person for the reasons behind your hatred, but rather surrender the hatred rising within you. If you have difficulty finding and focusing on the rising hatred within you, surrender it by reciting *Mirŭk Chon Yŏrae Pul* to the face of the one you hate or to his or her name.

Otherwise, invoke a wŏn to Buddha for the person you hate. Until the hatred in you disappears, invoke such wŏns as: "May_____ awaken the faith and reverence within himself, so that he can plant great merit before Buddha, parwŏn, I offer this wŏn." Since the mind wishing the hated person to accumulate great merit is your own mind, you will accumulate the merit before the other person does. Accumulating merit makes you more generous and gentle, and your mind does not become too sharp or bitter.

There was a man who detested his coworker. The presence of this coworker was like a thorn in his eye. And because the hatred was mutual, the man suffered unspeakably while working with that person. He once came to visit Master Baek and told him his problem, and Master Baek instructed him to invoke a wŏn for his coworker. So, according to Master Baek's teachings, he invoked this wŏn to Buddha: "May_____ awaken faith and devotion to Buddha, so that he can serve Buddha well, parwŏn."

Because the pain of his hatred was unbearable, he had to carry out the practice many times a day. Sometimes he invoked that wŏn to Buddha over a hundred times a day. After trying this for a year, he finally cleansed his mind of the hatred. His coworker no longer offended him so much, and he was at peace. Also, since he had opened his heart to Buddha every time he invoked his wŏns, he was full of joy.

The other person, however, was still experiencing the suffering of hell from his own hatred because he did not know how to cultivate his mind. Instead, to let out his repressed hatred, he quietly began criticizing the student of Master Baek who had cultivated his mind. If a third person were to see these two, the one who had cultivated his mind would appear virtuous, while the one who had not cultivated his mind would seem to be a narrow-minded person who only saw others' faults.

He who serves Buddha cultivates his mind by always watching his mind. He does not quarrel with any right or wrong outside of his mind.

HOLY TEACHER TULLE

AN OLD MAN named Tulle was often hired to work at Sosa Monastery. He gave us a hard time by taking advantage of our lack of knowledge in farming (for we were from Seoul) and of the fact that he had been living in that area longer than we. He tricked us in many ways and worked carelessly while still receiving his full salary.

As a spiritual seeker who had devoted my life to Buddha, I felt I could not forgive his dishonest attitude. I was in charge of the kitchen back then. At the immature age of twenty-six, I could not bear the discomfort of serving such precious food to such a despicable person. Also, because he treated us—those who were training for the path of enlightenment—as laborers like himself and tried to act as our superior, his arrogance seemed ridiculous to me. He was like a thorn in my eye.

Since I could not stand him whenever I saw him, I was forced to intensely surrender my painful hatred by reciting *Miruk Chon Yorae Pul.* For fifteen days, I surrendered every hatred that rose within me without letting any of it escape. One day, out of nowhere, I heard a voice saying, "Holy teacher Tulle, holy teacher Tulle." The voice was rich and majestic.

Tulle, the one who caused me to surrender my wicked hatred, was truly a holy teacher to me. I felt thankful to him again and again, for without him, I probably could not have purified this hateful mind of mine.

It is people like him who are my Buddhas. All people who awaken me or make me cultivate my mind are my Buddhas. Where else would you look for Buddhas? If a person truly realizes that everyone is a Buddha at peace, such a person is probably also a Buddha at peace.

THE PERSON WHO ENLIGHTENS ME
IS MY BUDDHA

THERE WAS A MONK who used to hate cleaning and kitchen duties, but after the abbot of his monastery made him do those chores during his one-hundred-day meditation retreat, those tasks became enjoyable to him. This was a result of cleansing his mind of the dislike for work.

How fortunate he is now that he has no aversion to his duties and is full of joy! Because there is that much less distaste in his mind, his body has become much more cheerful. For that monk, the abbot of the monastery who forced him to do the work and made him cultivate his mind by doing so is his Buddha.

People who enlighten me are all my Buddhas. Instead of trying to find Buddhas in high and precious places, shouldn't you be able to find your Buddhas in your town, in your marketplaces, and in your streets? Everyone has valuable and enlightening qualities. If you learned and practiced those qualities, it would be like meeting the Buddha and practicing his teachings. There are plenty of Buddhas around us all the time: Buddhas in our homes, Buddhas at our workplaces, Buddhas in our streets, and Buddhas in our buses...

SURRENDERING
THE ATTACHMENT TO THE BODY

IN THE PROCESS OF CLEANSING my basic karmic hindrances, I was scolded and often hit by my teacher. It wounded my pride as a senior practitioner, especially when he scolded me harshly in front of the other practitioners. I did not know how to deal with the embarrassment and the humiliation. The sorrow and discontent rising sharply within me only caused more pain.

At those times, if I kept staring at my painful mind and surrendered it by reciting *Mirŭk Chon Yŏrae Pul*, the one who was getting scolded did not feel like me, but someone else. Eventually, I stopped becoming embarrassed and hurt by my teacher's scolding. Such equanimity was evidence that my sharply arising ego was melting away through the practice of surrendering.

Even on hot summer days, when my mind could not tolerate the heat, I surrendered my discomfort and it lessened the pain. The heat then became bearable. It may have been a little hot out, but I no longer had to put up with my suffocating annoyance.

One time I was sitting in the ditches of a bean field, pulling up weeds the day after it had rained. It felt as if the heat would suffocate me—not the slightest breeze blew along the ditch. On top of that, the heat rose up from the ground, and the sun's rays struck on my back. It was one o'clock in the afternoon, the hottest time of the day.

At that moment, while I intensely surrendered the notion that the heat was unbearable, sweat began to drip from my head down my back, running down the trough of my spine like cool refreshing raindrops on my skin. If the heat of anger is in your mind, you cannot bear any additional heat from outside. But, since I was surrendering the stuffy heat in my mind as soon as it came up, the heat was not accumulating in me. Therefore, I did not feel as much pain.

During the seven and a half years of my life at Sosa, between 12:00 P.M. and 3:00 P.M. of every hot summer day, I overcame the heat—while carrying a heavy rack on my back, while cutting grass, while pulling weeds, while tilling the soil, and while pulling carts. I did not give in to my mind when it complained about the heat. Even during the middle of the day, my working mentality was one of continual surrendering—even when my sweaty clothes stuck to my body, leaving me sticky and disgusting, the practice of surrendering continued. It was a practice that dealt fiercely with my ego.

Once I milked a cow while taking in its steamy body heat with my whole body—my upper body pressed against the cow's leg and my forehead pressed against her stomach. It was unbearable at that moment. After doing the same with three more cows, I had no strength left in my hands and arms. My shirt was full of sweat, as if it had been soaked in water. On top of that, when the cow used its manure-caked tail to chase away the flies and whipped my face and eyes instead, it quickly stirred up my disgust and my ego. Those tense moments—my face covered with cow manure and sweat pouring out of me like raindrops, milking a cow with a bucket between my knees to protect it from being kicked over—those were important moments in the cultivation of my mind.

This practice of surrendering while working, constantly surrendering more and more, is itself the very reverence that speaks "Lord Buddha." In this reverence, there is not even an "I" who generates reverence. The worst conditions then become ideal conditions for cultivating one's mind.

Once, I put too much cow dung on my rack, and I could barely get up and keep my balance because my legs were so shaky. I had to carry the rack of dung over a hill with an incline of almost twenty degrees to a field about two-thirds of a mile away from the monastery. Since I was used to taking the rack there without stopping, I tried to surrender the feeling of discomfort from the heavy load and to arrive without stopping. Meanwhile, my body was crying out in pain. Step by step, with all my strength, I surrendered the burden of that heavy load while fiercely asking myself, "What is the true nature of this thing that's complaining about the heavy

POLISHING THE DIAMOND, ENLIGHTENING THE MIND

load?" It was a matter of life and death. Not once did I give in to myself. Because I was consistently able to surrender the attachment to my body, my mind was like a never-losing battlefield.

Sometimes, as I carried crops from the distant fields or walked down the dark mountain path by myself at night, it felt as if someone were pulling me from behind. When my whole body became overwhelmed by the dark energy from behind, I looked straight ahead and surrendered the horrible feeling of wanting to look back. If too much fear arose in my mind, I knelt and surrendered it on the spot by reciting *Mirŭk Chon Yŏrae Pul* for at least thirty minutes. I then descended the mountain with a peaceful mind. In the winter, I surrendered while kneeling on top of the ice-covered path in the mountains. I held out with the attitude of "Here, take this body if you want!" and surrendered my fear. When I came down from the mountain after surrendering my fear, I felt extremely happy.

When I used to think of my mother, who became a widow at twenty-three, my heart felt as if it were being torn apart. I was the second generation of only-sons, and my one sister had gone to Germany, leaving my mother alone in our hometown. This was a strong attachment, a blood tie, and being able to surrender the karmic attachment of blood ties is very important for spiritual seekers. Sexual desire can be surrendered relatively easily without losing mindfulness, because such desire can be embarrassing, but karmic ties to a parent, especially to a widowed mother, are hard indeed to surrender. When I was finally freed from that karmic attachment, the world became simply refreshing, tranquil, and bright. My doubts were resolved and insightful wisdom arose.

There is power that comes from overcoming attachment to one's body. This power leads to eradicating doubts and knowing the true nature of things. Realizations come naturally through the practice of surrendering.

PURIFY ANGER TO ACHIEVE BUDDHAHOOD

T HERE IS A SAYING, "Purify yourself of anger to achieve Buddha-hood." Anger should be completely cleansed from the mind. However, surrendering anger is as painful as tearing out one's heart.

I had so much trouble surrendering my anger at Sosa. Every time anger from my past lives surfaced, it was hell beyond comparison. For an entire day, my mind would be upset, my inner body would burn, and I was full of complaints. Since my mind was burning, my face also burned darkly. Whatever I did, my mind was not at ease, and it was constantly bubbling up. Even the sound of the wind, the sound of a door being slammed, or even someone smiling, angered me.

For people who do not have much anger in them, this is probably hard to understand. Even though they live on the same land and in the same environment, heavenly beings and hellish beings are divided according to the state of their minds. One group lives in happiness, and the other lives in constant complaint, hatred, and spite.

One time I surrendered an angry mind as if my life depended on it. The anger surfaced in me while I was working in the field, and I sat down on the spot, focused my vision, and stopped my breathing. I was worried that, if I remained standing, the feeling of too much wind on my legs, body, and head would destroy my concentration, or that my vision might be too wide and distract me from my surrendering. So I sat and looked down. Also, since the sound of my breathing might break my concentration, I concentrated my mind and body on a single extended breath and fiercely surrendered the anger in me by reciting *Mirŭk Chon Yŏrae Pul.* Since the sound of reciting might distract my surrendering, I recited silently. By surrendering with such strong determination, I was able to take care of the anger with two or three long breaths. In one breath, I focused on reciting *Mirŭk Chon Yŏrae Pul* more than ten times, as if I were focusing sunlight through a convex lens to burn a piece of paper.

When you practice your surrendering like this, the root of the anger gets cleansed, and your heart feels very refreshed. Because anger is an emotion to which you have been conditioned, if you surrender it to Buddha's radiance every time it arises, you can liberate yourself from it. Furthermore, as you sense the Buddha's realm of light, your wisdom-eye will open and you will perceive the true nature of things. Once you overcome the root of your anger, the realm of wisdom will open up for you, and the bright and refreshing Dharma bliss will lead to pure reverence. I am so grateful that there is a Buddha who will accept this suffering from me.

Lord Buddha, Master Baek, if it were not for the method of surrendering that you realized, how could I have ever surrendered that mind of anger? I thank you!

THE BURNING FIRE

ONCE, WHEN LORD BUDDHA was passing by a mountain with his students, a fire started on the mountain. The crackling red-hot fire gave off a scorching heat. Buddha then lectured:

"Monks, there is a fire that is hotter than that flame on the mountain. It is the fire that burns in your mind called the fire of lust. The fire that burns fiercely on the mountain only burns your body. But the fire of lust—raging in your mind, desiring beautiful women—burns your mind, too." As Buddha let out his lion's roar, some were greatly awakened, some threw up blood, and some ran away.

Buddha also said that if there were one more thing like sexual desire, no one would attain Buddhahood. Overcoming sexual desire was difficult back then, and it is difficult now. Since sexual desire originates within the mind, however, by surrendering that craving mind to Buddha, you can, in the end, be liberated even from that mind.

If you restrain or suppress your sexual desires too much, though, it can cause harmful side effects to the body. And if a spiritual seeker mutilates his body because he cannot handle his sexual desires, it is hard for him to become enlightened due to the regret that he imprints on the mind. We should simply surrender arising desires with great reverence. One who controls his mind and body by surrendering his desires is, indeed, an able person.

CHECK THE DOOR LOCK
AT THE THIRD HOUR

A MONASTERY'S FRONT GATE and fences help to guard spiritual seekers' minds. The mind that practices the three poisons of greed, anger, and ignorance always directs its attention outside the monastery. Gates and fences, however, present a psychological barrier to such distractions. The notion that one is closed in weakens and blocks the karmic force.

The saying "check the door lock at the third hour of the night" started in reference to disciplining the mind. Master Baek always barred the door and locked the padlock. Even on hot summer days, he slept with his door closed. He always closed the door whenever he went in or out of the room, and he told us to do the same. He taught us this habit as an aid in cultivating the mind.

In cultivating one's mind, monastic rules work as gates and fences. The rules are not to tie people down but to discipline the karmic hindrance that distracts them from their practice. Following the rules gives rise to stability, and stability gives rise to wisdom. By swiftly surrendering the mind that wants to escape the rules, and also by surrendering the mind that wants to follow the rules, your mind becomes healthy and free before the rules. And from freedom your actions will find order.

T HE BRIGHT ENERGY of the universe starts to rise at three in the morning and lasts till three in the afternoon. So at 3 A.M. the sky is dark but
the energy is bright, and at 3 P.M. the sky is bright but the energy is dark.
Since our minds also change with the energy of the universe, our minds
are clear in the morning but they become cloudy in the afternoon.

When 9 P.M. approaches, negative energy starts to circulate. That is
why offerings to spirits are usually made after 9 P.M., and that is also why
monks in the monasteries go to bed around 9 P.M. At around 3 A.M. the
negative energy begins to disappear, and between 3 A.M. and 5 A.M., the
energy is very bright and clear. The Bodhisattva Manjushri is said to
hold his Dharma lectures during these hours. When you get up at this
hour to practice, you will receive the energy of the universe in full.

It is said that among the ones who get up early in the morning there
is rarely a person who is not bright, and among the ones who roam
around late at night there is rarely a person who does not face misfortune.
By following the energy of the universe—working when there is bright
energy and sleeping when the energy is dark—our minds and bodies will
become healthy.

For those who cultivate the mind, it is better not to lose the mindfulness of reciting *Mirŭk Chon Yŏrae Pul* before falling asleep. By doing
so, practice continues throughout the night until the moment you wake
up. On the other hand, if you fall asleep in an absentminded state, you
will remain absentminded throughout your sleep, and your mind will
not be clear even when you wake up.

In our monastery, we sleep with the lights on in every room. The reason is to imprint brightness in our minds instead of darkness, helping us
in our efforts to enlighten our minds. It is preferable, also, not to take naps
during the day, for then you are practicing the dark mind on a bright day.

DISCRIMINATING MINDS
OCCUR IN UNITS OF THREES

AMONG THE DISCRIMINATIONS in our minds, some occur every three seconds, some every three minutes, some every thirty minutes, three hours, three days, three weeks, three months, or three hundred years. There are even discriminations that occur every three thousand years.

If you miss your chance to surrender a discrimination that occurs every three thousand years, your attainment of Buddhahood gets delayed for another three thousand years. One who has cleansed himself of all his discriminations is a Buddha. Losing the chance to purify from one's mind an inner discrimination that occurs only every three hundred years is also a terrible mistake. You should always be mindful lest you lose your chance to surrender to Buddha the precious offerings that arise only once every couple of lifetimes.

The essence and the life of practice is not losing the chance to surrender the discriminations, which arise and sink in units of three. When a thought arises, you have one more thing to cleanse from your mind, for if you do not cleanse that thought now, you will have to do it in your next life.

While I was training at Sosa, every time I was wrestling with a karmic hindrance that had arisen in me, my teacher would admonish me, saying, "If you do that now (struggle with it), it will be a burden in your next life." In other words, if I did *not* struggle, but surrendered it instead, it would become the job of this life. He was telling us to solve the "one great aim [of becoming enlightened]" in this very life.

SEE YOUR OWN FACE
AND SURRENDER YOUR FAULTS

BUDDHA'S EYES are called the eyes of the blue lotus. It is said that if your mentality is that of covering up others' flaws as if they were your own flaws and of disclosing your flaws as if they were others' flaws, then your eyes will look like those of Buddha, wherein the middle of the eye seems slightly closed, and the ends seem slightly open. On the other hand, if your mind is full of the desire to find others' faults, your eyes will be as round as jawbreaker candies—just like a cat's eyes when it is trying to find a mouse.

There are many theories about how one's mentality influences one's physical attributes. It is said, for instance, that if a person has a sharp nose line, his mind is like the sharp edge of a sword. Thus, if he intends to strike someone down and fails to do so, his mind will hit himself back, causing him, in many cases, to have bad lungs. A person with a less forgiving mind is said to have a narrow space between his eyebrows. Such a person should use his mind more gently and generously and practice a forgiving and understanding mind to others. Moreover, a person with high cheekbones is said to be opinionated; a person with a straight nose bridge is said to have an honest personality; a person who is cross-eyed is said to have a hard time concentrating his or her mind on one thing; someone's whose face is very dark is said to be very greedy, and so on.

The facial features come from the skull features, and the skull features come from the mind's features. In order for your facial features to change, the way you use your mind should change. In the end, people advertise "I live my life this way" with their faces.

By the time we reach age twenty-seven, through regeneration, even our brain cells have changed, and we have completely different bodies than the ones our parents gave us. We have become totally independent of our parents. Therefore our faces after twenty-seven are not our parents' fault. The way we use our minds continues the building of our faces.

Four

Be True

to the Present Present

BE TRUE TO THE PRESENT PRESENT

THE PAST HAS ALREADY GONE BY, the future is not yet here, and as soon as we say, "the present" it has already become our past. We should be true to each passing moment, which we cannot even truly call "the present."

Because elderly people are attached to the past and live in their memories, thinking, "In the good old days things used to be…," they practice the dead mind. Likewise, young people have only grand blueprints for their future and lack the present foundation from which to gradually fulfill their plans. They practice the delusive mind.

He who can surrender the discriminations that are arising this very moment, who can solve the problem right in front of him without avoiding it, is one who can utilize the present in the present. Such a person is indeed an able person. If you are true to your present present, you will naturally be true to your future future, and you will be true to your past past.

If you do not postpone today's job until tomorrow, quarrel over the right or wrong of yesterday's incident, nor worry about tomorrow's job ahead, then the calm and vitality arising in your mind will make your present more meaningful.

Living one hundred years a day is a sign of an ignorant person. Regretting things that happened five years ago and worrying about things that won't happen until five years from now is a foolishness that should be avoided by a household of spiritual seekers. How fulfilling it would be if we were able to live just twenty-four hours a day! It is difficult to live even twenty-four hours a day, but how peaceful and serene our minds would be if we were able to live just twelve hours a day! As the clock endlessly ticks away, how many of us recognize the gravity of our inability to turn back time? This very moment disappears forever.

To the enlightened mind—which arises from eradicating the discrimination of time that stretches for eons—there is only the present, and the present, which lives in the big present [which encompasses the past, present, and future], is the entire universe. This present is freed from even the chronological characteristic of a beginning and an ending. Whether it is the present of three thousand years ago or the present of this moment, the root is the same: the One Mind. Thus the present is the entire body of life itself, and the moment you are awakened to the present, it is simply enlightenment.

The present might even be the Buddha. The truthful mind is the moment in which the Buddha dwells. When Buddha is enshrined in a mind, that mind's speech and actions are reverent—its behavior is dignified and its spirit is always awake.

Therefore, awaken to the present. Becoming enlightened by being true to the present present is the finest tranquillity.

MINDING THE STORE

W HEN YOU ARE RUNNING A STORE and business is lagging, instead of being troubled by the lack of customers, you should surrender that troubled feeling. As long as you are stuck with a troubled mind, the mental wave it creates will completely fill the store with an annoying energy. Even if a customer wanted to come in and shop, he or she would sense the negative wave, for human minds are that sensitive, and the customer would lose interest and not go in. And if a customer did come in, the negative wave would make him or her leave quickly.

Surrendering feelings of annoyance and worry is the practice that will attract customers. If you do not let your mind wander or worry, you will be bright and awake, and you can dust the store or organize the merchandise. In the moment you are busy working, your mind is diligent and alive. An alive mind's wave generates vibrant energy, and such energy motivates customers to shop at your store. Even if customers do not come right away, with an alive mind, wisdom and calm arise to solve the problem and look for new possibilities.

An alive mind achieves tangible success in life. The human world is established on the consequences of numerous alive minds. Various colors filled with vibrant energy are brightly leading the world of reality. If business is slow in a rice store, isn't it better if the owner picks the dust from the rice and changes the display of his merchandise to attract some attention to the store, rather than doing nothing and letting his thoughts wander? When an atmosphere of diligence is alive in a store, customers come, attracted by that diligence. This is the businessman's mind practicing being true to the present.

Thinking one's business is slow should also absolutely be avoided. You should avoid even letting those words out of your mouth. When others ask you how business is, it is better for you to tell them that it is going well. Indeed, you yourself should actually have the mentality that your business is going well. In the end, being successful depends on the conditioning of your mind.

NOT LOSING YOUR MINDFULNESS

A COUPLE OF DAYS AGO, I heard that someone was walking down the stairs drunk, with his hands in his pockets, and fell down the stairs and died from head injuries. As this example shows, absentmindedness should absolutely be avoided. One who tries to be true to the present would be just as alert walking down the stairs as when he was walking up the stairs. Every time you take a step, you should retain the mindfulness of surrendering by reciting *Miruk Chon Yŏrae Pul.* Just in case, you should be prepared to put your hands out. It helps you in cultivating your mind, and it eliminates any danger.

Also, before we go meet someone, we usually ponder about how we are going to answer if he or she says this or that, and we think about going to certain places with him or her. However, when we actually meet the person, so many times we learn that our pondering was useless, and the situation ends up being totally different from what we had expected. Every time your mind ponders, imagining what is going to happen, surrender those thoughts. Instead of following such drifting thoughts, if you keep surrendering those thoughts and reach the nondual state, you might become aware of what is actually going to happen in your meeting. Your mind becomes brighter, giving you the appropriate answers to the other person's questions. Also, your mind's power becomes clear and strong enough to help put him or her at ease.

A POSITIVE MENTALITY

WHEN SOMEONE ASKS US a favor, we usually give a clear "yes" or "no" right away without much consideration. Some matters should be handled in such a way, but if we are always that careless, we might suffer a loss or hurt someone's feelings.

When someone makes a request, a generous person first accepts that person's feelings by communicating, "Yes, I want to help you!" A person with a negative mind, however, initially rejects the request as an imposition. A negative person resists other people's feelings, and there are several possible explanations why. It might be because the negative person is arrogant and does not try to learn from others, or because he is close-minded. If he is angry and unstable, he may simply not have enough sense to accept them. In any case, if the necessary conditions are not there, he does not willingly accept the other person's feelings. If a person starts, however, by constantly practicing the positive mentality of saying, "yes!" then the positive action of saying, "yes" comes naturally.

Whether or not you actually end up carrying out the favor for the other person, he will be satisfied and his mind will be calmed if you first accept his feelings. Since human minds are typically weak, a rejection of his feelings will cause vengeance to surge in his mind. When such a poisonous mind is provoked, isn't it painful for everyone? An accomplished person is able to embrace such a mind, to soothe it, and give it different perspectives.

The accepting mind is the mind that wants to satisfy the other person. By practicing such a mentality, many possibilities for exchanging virtue between yourself and the other person arise. Because you have accepted the other's feelings by saying, "yes!", if you then say, "Let's think of the possibilities," the other person will be content. If there is a possibility, the other person's request will be fulfilled. What happens, however, when what the other has asked turns out to be impossible? Since you first said,

"Let's think of the possibilities," then, when the other person responds, you can tell him or her, "I am in such and such a situation" and ask, "What do you think I should do?" In this way, you can resolve the situation regardless of the end result, neither of your feelings would be hurt, and the intended goal would be accomplished.

Solving these types of problems with humility is called the housekeeping of one's mind.

THE MIND THAT SHELTERS
NO IMPOSSIBILITIES

I ONCE KNEW A PERSON who ran a rice mill. At this mill, whenever I saw the strong workers easily picking up large sacks of rice, I used to think, "I should be able to do that," and I became envious of them. I knew that there was no way I could lift a sack of rice with my limited strength at that time. So every time I saw a sack of rice, I endlessly surrendered my sense of impossibility by reciting *Mirŭk Chon Yŏrae Pul.*

One day, one of the sacks of rice appeared very small to me. I lifted it up and threw it, and it landed far away. Everyone around looked at me with shocked expressions. Since I had been surrendering the notions of heaviness, to the extent that I had surrendered those notions, that much Dharma power had been awakened in me. With that Dharma power, I was able to throw the sack of rice.

If you pass on to the next life with a belief in your inability to do a certain thing, then in your next life, you still will not be able to do that thing. Without even talking about the life to come, if you practice the mind of impossibility in this life, even things that are possible now will become impossible. When you surrender the notion of both possibility and impossibility to Buddha, however, and face your problems without any preconceived notions, you will be able to accomplish your goals naturally.

BE FREE FROM PRECONCEIVED NOTIONS

ONCE A MAN CAME to see Master Baek at Sosa and said, "I can't breathe too well, sir." Our teacher told him, "Surrender the mind that believes you can't breathe too well to Buddha, and breathe as much as you want." The man had been suffering from tuberculosis for a long time and his asthma had caused difficulties in breathing, but after he had visited our teacher, his asthma improved. Prior to his visit, he was not able to breathe well simply because of the single notion that he could not breathe well.

Likewise, one whose single notion is loneliness is always lonely. One whose single notion is poverty is always poor. One whose single notion is that of a beggar lives his entire life as a beggar. One whose single notion is arrogance always thinks that he or she is superior to everyone else. Since such a person does not try to learn from either the wise or the world, he or she runs into many failures.

A third grader lives with a third grader's wisdom, knowledge, and use of the mind. If he believes his thoughts are always correct, he will not try to become a fourth grader. He won't let go of his third grade level of thought because of his ego. At the same time, he believes his level is that of a sixth grader, with a sixth grader's knowledge and wisdom. He flaunts himself as a sixth grader, only to despair after running into the cold reality. In such despair, he may conclude that fate is cruel.

The wisdom that realizes your limitations should lead the way to straightening out your crooked mind, deepening your shallow mind, widening your narrow mind, and enlightening your darkened mind. By knowing that all human preconceived notions are mistaken and by surrendering them, your wisdom will grow.

We judge others with our preconceived notions of them from the past couple of years. How dangerous that is! Even though the other person has changed through time and space, and he or she is not the same person of a few years before, we still judge him or her with our preconceived notions. We do not know the present person at all. If you surrender your preconceived notions about another, as well as your notions of him or her from the present moment, you will become aware of the other's true identity.

HELL IS WHEN YOU HAVE A STRONG EGO

A PERSON WITH A STRONG EGO expects to be greeted first when he runs into a person of inferior status; otherwise, he feels ashamed. A person with a strong ego would also feel ashamed if his spiritual progress were slower than that of his fellow practitioners, especially if he had started the practice earlier than they. The stronger the ego, the more inferior he feels to an accomplished person. His face blushes from shame.

If you do not think of others as inferior and try instead to learn from them, if you do not think that you started spiritual practice earlier but instead believe that everyone is equal before Buddha, then you will find nothing of which to be ashamed. If you have practiced for, say, one year or for ten years, your brightness may be like a thirty-watt bulb or like a five-hundred-watt bulb. Next to the sunrise, however, both light bulbs would seem dim. Surrender the notion that you have been practicing longer than others, for in the sunlight all other lights are equal.

If your state of mind is one of serving Buddha, there is no suffering from a strong ego, because in reverent service the "I" is not allowed. In that moment of reverent service, everything is heavenly and bright, and the "I," which is only the physical body and suffering, cannot arise.

ONLY MY MOTHER

Ιғ ʏοu wιsнед for your mother to be only your mother—to be neither your father's wife, nor your siblings' mother, nor your grandmother's daughter, nor your aunt's sister—if you wished for her to be only your mother, to take care of only you, then she would become miserable.

A child suffers the most when its parents' love is taken away by his or her newborn sibling. This is not only true with children. It is the same with a student who wants the sole attention of his teacher or an employee who desires the sole trust of his employer. By recognizing, however, that they are everyone's teacher, everyone's elder, everyone's Buddha, you will be able to cleanse the attachment to "only mine." When you cleanse the notion of "only mine," and when you realize that you are equal to all people, your wisdom tree will grow.

Only when you support your mother in her roles as your father's wife, your grandmother's daughter, and your siblings' mother will she become greater than "only my mother."

WE USUALLY LIVE OUR LIVES with the belief that "I sacrifice myself for everyone else," rather than thinking that "everyone else helps me." We believe that we pay taxes and go to tedious town meetings for our society and our nation. We focus on all the things we do for our families. With this attitude, many housewives begin to regret their lives when they reach old age. They ask for compensation for the youth they spent taking care of their family. Such people think that they are the only ones who have sacrificed for their families. They believe that only their lives are miserable.

If you are such a person, look back and see how lonely your life would have been without your husband and your children! Your husband was a guide through your rough life, a friend who talked to you during your spiritual hardships. Your children are not the burden of your life. See how meaningful and rich your life has been simply because they exist!

Usually parents think that they have to earn a living to raise their children, and they say, "I worked so hard to raise and educate my children." But a Chinese sage once said, "Heaven gave a name to the grass when it created the grass, and food to humans when it created them." This means that a person is born with a certain collection of merit, and no matter what kind of household he is born into, the condition of his life really depends on that merit. These days there are too many children with too much worldly merit—their parents race around doing errands, providing for them. Then again, there probably are parents who live well because of their children's merit.

Looking back on the Vietnamese boat people who had no country, who died on small boats out of exhaustion, we are reminded of our country's service to us. Before dwelling on the idea that we pay taxes to run the country, think instead how grateful we should feel that our country protects us. Let's try and practice the grateful mind to the world that helps us.

DO NOT STOP PEOPLE FROM COMING TO YOU, NOR STOP THEM FROM LEAVING YOU

A POSALLIM HAD JUST BEGAN the practice of reading the Diamond Sutra. Her son, who was attending a prominent university, had completely lost himself in the student movement, wandering around leading demonstrations, completely neglecting his school work. The posallim became so worried about him that she could not eat anything, and she soon fell ill with a stomach disease. She had four children, but the boy was her only son, and the whole family had high expectations of him. Since he was liable to be arrested anytime for leading student protests, the family was full of fear and anxiety, as if there had been a death in the family. Nonetheless, he would not change his ways. Even when his favorite sister tried to change his mind, he would not listen, and his mother's pleas were of no use.

She asked me, "What should I do?" I told her to draw her son's face in her mind and practice surrendering by reciting *Mirŭk Chon Yŏrae Pul* to his face, while offering a wŏn to Buddha and reading the Diamond Sutra seven times a day. She practiced exactly as I told her. Three days after she had started the practice, she was reciting *Mirŭk Chon Yŏrae Pul* one night, and at about 3:30 in the morning she had a vision of her son lingering around the Seoul train station with messy hair, wearing ragged clothes and holding a small bag.

The next afternoon, her son came down from Seoul without any notice. Suddenly the whole house was in a festive mood. Later, the son set his path on his studies again and became a prizewinning student.

A few months later, the posallim came to see me again. Her oldest daughter was twenty-nine and the second oldest was twenty-seven. She said that their not being married was a big problem for her, and she let out a sigh as big as Tai Shan Mountain in China.

I told her to offer a wŏn to Buddha by saying, "May my daughter meet a good husband so that they may serve Buddha well, parwŏn." And once again she diligently read the sutra, offered the wŏn to Buddha, and practiced surrendering. One month later, her eldest daughter's marriage came through. Through the force of her wŏn, which she had cultivated both in her previous lives and in this lifetime, the realities of her life changed.

Let's say that a person is invoking a wŏn with the power of three hundred volts, and the person who tells him or her to make that wŏn—the one who makes the decision—has a wŏn with a power of one thousand volts. With the spark of their two wills coming together, they bring out the force of thirteen hundred volts. There is hardly anything that cannot be achieved with this kind of strength. In fact, since the end result of the wish is "to serve Buddha well," there is nothing that cannot be achieved. One thing to keep in mind is that you must trust the person who is making the decision for you to invoke the wŏn, and you have to follow his or her directions. Only then will the wŏn you invoke before Buddha be achieved.

When, in accord with her wishes, the posallim had finally married off her daughter, she felt so depressed and empty that she could not get up for three days. The posallim's relationship with her husband hadn't been very good, and she had always depended on her eldest daughter for advice and friendship. She was used to discussing family problems with her. Upon finding a husband, however, the daughter left her mother without any regret. The mother grieved, "What can compensate me for my lost years? If I had known this would happen in the end, I would have used my life instead to follow the spiritual path and solve the problem of birth and death." She felt her whole life had been meaningless and in vain.

The aim of spiritual practice is to make your mind healthy. If you are accomplished in your training and help others with your mind, you will feel secure. But if you help others while your mind is still weak, your mind loses itself in the hope of a reward, and you become just an empty shell. From a healthy self, there is a healthy family, and from a healthy family there is a healthy nation.

When you do not block people from coming to you, when you do not stop people from leaving, and when your mind transcends both their coming and leaving, your spiritual practice is indeed accomplished.

Five

May You Accumulate
Much Merit

———

DON'T JUST HOPE TO BE WELL OFF,
PLANT THE CAUSES TO BE WELL OFF

EVERYONE WANTS to be well off. However, we first must plant the causes of prosperity in order to achieve the desired effect. Always invoke a wŏn to plant merit. If you then actually practice planting merit, you will be well off as a result.

*If you invoke a wŏn, the container that holds
your merit will become bigger*

Heaven bestows rain evenly, but a cup can only hold a cupful, a bowl can only hold a bowlful, and a washbowl can only hold a washbowlful. The water overflows if there is more rain than the vessel can hold. If you invoke a wŏn to plant merit, your container of merit will grow. Invoking wŏns to plant much merit before Buddha means that you are making a vow to create opportunities by yourself—to actually plant merit—so that you may serve Buddha well.

Saving becomes merit

If our mentality is to be thrifty with the material goods that are the rewards of our precious labor, we plant merit. We should practice the thrifty mentality of conserving water, food, household furniture, and so on. We should also practice the mind of fixing items that are broken and of saving surplus goods to give them to those who need them.

Carefully saving your wages plants blessed fortune, too. Through doing so, your container of merit will grow. You do not accumulate merit by squandering money. If you spend money too freely, your good fortune will leave you.

You should not carelessly throw away food, such as rice. Often, house-wives accumulate merit by serving food to their families, then nullify their merits by throwing away the leftovers. Whether it is water or electricity, if your mentality is that of regarding all things as valuable, if your mind is thrifty, then it immediately becomes merit.

Accumulate your merit aggressively

Merit is not something that you pray for. You have to aggressively plant merit, and you only receive as much as you have planted. You cannot give your merit to someone else, nor can you receive someone else's. By transcending the boundary of self through the mentality of serving and sacrificing for family, neighbors, and society, you plant merit. The everyday practice of trying to help others with your giving mind becomes merit for your future.

Of course, by starting a project to serve Buddha—such as building temples, printing sutras, and so on—or by participating in such a project, you plant much merit, too. If someone accumulates merit from serving Buddha in whatever way, even after many incarnations he will be successful in the area in which he has accumulated his merit.

Sometimes, simply producing certain thoughts directly becomes merit for you, for example: revering Buddha with utmost devotion, wanting Buddha's bright Dharma to continue forever in *samsara*, revering all spiritual seekers, and wishing that they all attain enlightenment.

By cultivating your mind, you aid others with the radiance of your enlightenment. This becomes great merit, merit that makes the Buddha happy.

Prevent misfortune to retain your merit

Preventing misfortune is just as important as physically and spiritually planting merit. If a disaster strikes you, it can put a hole in the container that holds your merit. Just as water leaks through a bowl's crack, so too will your merit seep out.

For example, you could lose the merit that produces your material wealth through misfortune, and lose all your wealth through theft, fire, or illness. There are also many spiritual misfortunes that can obstruct your progress toward enlightenment. Such misfortune occurs as a result of bad karma accumulated in your past lives, or negative karmic ties with other people.

Therefore, if you read the Diamond Sutra day and night and surrender your arising minds well, without losing your mindfulness, you will free yourself from such misfortune. Then, the merit that is contained in your vessel will be maintained.

GREAT MERIT OF NO LIMIT

YOU MIGHT SAY that a person who owns a lot of material goods, who spends money like water, and who lives in an expensive house is blessed with much merit. However, you cannot call his or her merit "the great merit of no limit." When someone has the great merit of no limit, this person might not have much material wealth in ordinary times, but when his need arises he will be able to acquire anything he wants. If you possess much material wealth, you have to worry about taking care of it and protecting it. But with the great merit of no limit fulfilling your needs at any time, you do not have such concerns. With such blessed fortune, if you think that you need some warm clothes for winter, you get clothes in a few days. Even with food, if you demand what you need with your mind, it comes to you automatically. It is the same with daily supplies. If you generate the mind of want, in a couple of days, either someone would tell you where it was, or you will obtain it.

There was once a person whose health was weakening. He thought, "I will have to get some medicine chicks, and prepare them with ginseng." A few days after he had such a thought, someone brought him ten medicine chicks.

For some children, every time their parents want to do something for them, it just doesn't work out. But for others, as soon as their parents generate a wish to do something for them, it works out easily. For the children who have planted merit in their past, every time the parents want to provide something for them, it is immediately accomplished.

The great merit of no limit means one's blessed fortune never runs out. If there are no needy, poverty-stricken feelings in one's mind at all, one's face shines with merit. That person has cleansed every sense of poverty from his or her mind and has planted great merit before Buddha.

You plant the great merit of no limit when you practice such attitudes as utmost reverence to Buddha, a deep desire to repay Buddha's grace, joy about Buddha's realm of light, and when you offer both your mind and body to Buddha to make him happy, and want to enlighten another's human nature to make Buddha happy, and so on.

SURRENDER EVEN YOUR MERIT

H E WHO CULTIVATES his mind is not greedy for merit. The merit that you plant will follow you anytime, anywhere, if you just pull at it like you would pull a yo-yo on a string.

If you generate the mentality of selfishly claiming your merit, your merit decreases. But if you surrender your merit to Buddha, you plant an even greater merit, and you imprint Buddha fully in your mind. At that instant, your mind comes closer to enlightenment, and your ego melts away.

We should surrender our intention to selfishly seek merit and recognition for our merit, and instead simply plant merit and cultivate wisdom.

YOU CANNOT GIVE YOUR MERIT
TO SOMEONE ELSE, NOR CAN YOU
ACCEPT SOMEONE ELSE'S MERIT

O NCE THE BUDDHA WENT to accept the offering of a meal from a certain king. The greedy king wanted to keep the merit of the offering all to himself, so he announced that, from the day the Buddha arrived in his kingdom, anyone coming before the king would be punished according to the law of the land. And every day, in preparation for the Buddha's arrival, the king had his chefs make enough food to feed hundreds of people.

The day the Buddha arrived in the country with his disciples, no one went to tell the king because no one wanted to disobey the country's law. Even the chef would not tell the king for fear of punishment. He just made new meals every day and threw them away, making them again and again only to throw them away again and again.

As a result, the Buddha and his students had to starve for many days. When a merchant who was passing by the area heard the news, he offered them half of the five hundred bushels of oats that he had prepared for horse feed. Venerable Ananda went to town with the oats and said, "The maiden who grinds these oats will become a princess in her next life."

When the ground oats were offered to the Buddha, the Buddha said, "Why didn't you say that she'll become a Buddha in her next life? Becoming a princess is only one incarnation's merit, but if you said that she would become a Buddha, she would have become a Buddha forever." Thus he pointed out Ananda's error.

The Buddha asked the Venerable Ananda to try some food that the Buddha had just removed from his mouth. When Ananda tasted the food that had been chewed by the Buddha, he found it sweet and very delicious. Ananda asked, "Why are these oats so delicious?" The Buddha replied, "Food that enters the mouth of one who has planted much merit smells and tastes this way." The Buddha explained that this was the working of a person who had the power of merit.

You cannot give your merit to someone else, nor can you accept someone else's merit. In a family with many children, we sometimes see that material wealth and love are concentrated on a particular child. That is because he or she has planted more merit than the rest of his or her siblings. As the saying goes, "The shadow of Suyang Mountain stretches for eighty *li*." Even if only one person has planted merit in a family, still many people benefit from the power of that merit. However, one cannot give one's merit away. We see this is true in cases where the father dies and the family declines. Likewise, when a daughter with powerful merit gets married and moves away, her maiden household declines, but her newlywed household becomes well off.

There can be no blessed fortune where none has been planted. We should constantly plant merit.

B OTH HUMANS AND ANIMALS live with worries about what they will subsist on in the future. Even wealthy people are not free from this psychological problem, because their minds are still poor.

Feeding oneself is a problem for everyone. Domesticated animals are absolutely loyal to their owners because their owners feed them. The debt of being fed is enormous. A cow struggles to not go to the slaughterhouse, but if its owner orders it to go, the cow will enter, reluctantly, because of its indebted mind. The cow eventually has to surrender its body, which has been raised on someone else's food, to the person who provided that food. The mind records all the actions of giving and receiving. In the end, it has to pay back its debt.

People live with this problem of the mind forever, worrying how they will survive in the future. This fear never ends. When you look into the mind of one who eats late at night, you will see that he or she overeats at that time because he or she is worried about being hungry in the morning. People crave higher positions because they want to be able to freely satisfy their basic desire—the desire for food. People bow before their superiors in the workplace. People grovel before powerful people. All these are actions of those who have not solved their worries about how they will support themselves in the future. Fear about how one will support oneself in the future arises not because there is no way of sustaining oneself, but because one's mind is poor.

PURIFY YOUR NEEDY MIND,
CULTIVATE YOUR PLENTIFUL MIND

OFTEN, PEOPLE WHO MANAGE household budgets feel very constrained. They feel constrained by how much money they can spend in a month. They plan their budgets with a sense of being limited by monthly wages and respond to the world with the single notion of not having enough money. How desperate their minds are, living as they do with such a sense of deficiency.

People say that there are beggars with wealth and beggars without wealth. One who always has a sense of lack, though he is wealthy, is called the beggar with wealth. Whether you are wealthy or not, if your mind is deficient, you will constantly imprint deficiency and poverty in your mind. And if you imprint such notions in your mind without purifying them, you will become poor in this life and in the next. Even if you are not wealthy right now, if your mind is a wealthy person's mind, then your material wealth will become plentiful following your plentiful mind.

Before I entered Sosa Monastery, I was trying to pay for my sister's education while in the midst of a difficult economic situation. To free me from my sense of lack, Master Baek taught me to invoke a wŏn to Buddha saying, "May I be able to make my teacher's life stable, par-wŏn!" Even though I did not have much material wealth then, every time I generated a wish to make an enlightened person's economic life stable, I was able to accumulate merit in my poor mind.

Usually, the face of one who has practiced a needy mind for one hundred days and the face of one who has practiced the plentiful mind for one hundred days are totally different. The power of merit and grace that radiates from the face of one with much merit is externally very different from that of the person with a needy mind.

Trivial thoughts accumulate one by one to form the foundation of your stability. You must surrender the needy mind and practice the plentiful mind.

NOT IMPRINTING POVERTY ON ONE'S MIND

IF YOU HAVE MONEY in your pocket, even borrowed money, you feel confident when you go out. If your pockets are empty, your mind is constrained by such worries as "What if I need to spend some money?" or "What if I have to treat someone I meet?" Having enough money when you go out helps enlighten your mind.

Whenever our teacher sent us to buy something from the store, he always gave us plenty of money. Also, whenever anyone was looking for something, my teacher was ready immediately to give what was needed. He had all sorts of tools handy—a hammer, a wrench, a wire cutter, and so on. He even kept various types of nails handy that we did not immediately need. He told us to buy plenty of daily supplies, so we wouldn't have any sense of deficiency, and to arrange the necessary supplies neatly where we could easily see them.

Our teacher helped us to cultivate the plentiful mind and always told us to put it into practice.

BLACK PUPPY

Master Baek lost his parents early in his life, and so he lived with his grandmother. Because he was involved in the Korean Independence movement since his youth, he was considered a subversive character by the Japanese police, who relentlessly pursued him. Thus he was usually not at home, but wandering here and there until he finally left for Shanghai.

Master Baek's grandmother and sister were left at home. His grandmother was always worried, because there were only women living in the house. Consequently, she always hung Master Baek's clothes outside to dry and put out his shoes on the stepping stone even though he wasn't home. She worried that, if people thought the house was occupied only by women, they would try to take advantage of them or try to rob them.

One day, Master Baek's grandmother took half a sack of rice over to one of her poor neighbors. Since it was unusual for her to do something like that, Master Baek asked her why she gave them the rice. She said that she was being generous to them in order to prevent them from taking advantage of her household, for they might think that it was a wealthy household without any men. Master Baek, even then in his youth, thought how great a merit she would have planted if she had just given the rice in hopes that her neighbors would have a warm meal, instead of worrying about getting hurt by them.

Later, after Master Baek had returned from his study in Germany, he entered Kŭmgang Mountain to devote himself to the spiritual practice, determined to stay there for ten years. But about eight years after he started his practice, he got a telegraph from home saying that he was to receive the family inheritance, for his grandmother had passed away. Even though it was an enormous amount of wealth, he did not go since it was during his retreat period.

The day after his ten-year retreat, he went back to his house in Seoul and saw that his grandmother had received a dog's body—she was rein-carnated as a black dog and was guarding the house. In his Dharma lecture, Master Baek said that she had received this dog's body and had returned to guard the house because she died with the determination to protect her wealth.

She had lived in fear that someone might hurt her, so she clung to her wealth and guarded it until she died. Yet the outcome was, at most, being born as a dog.

If we do not cling to things, whether spiritual or physical, but surrender them instead to Buddha and give them away to others, it would benefit us even more. People, however, usually cannot do that.

PALACE GRANDMOTHER

MASTER BAEK HAD AN AUNT who, because she was once a court lady at the palace, was called by her relatives the "palace grandmother." When she was nearing the end of her life, she wished to hand down her enormous wealth to Master Baek and kept sending people to inform him of her wish. But no matter how many times they came, Master Baek absolutely refused to inherit the wealth and did not even go to visit her.

Seeing this, one posallim asked the enlightened Master Son Hye-chŏng, "Why is Master Baek not even budging when many of his relatives, whom he rarely sees, come to give him this inheritance?" Master Son replied, "This is quite interesting." She said that Master Baek was trying to deliver his aunt.

The posallim then asked, "How is he going to lead her to her salvation?" Master Son explained to her that Master Baek's aunt had conditioned a strong attachment to wealth all her life. Now Master Baek was trying to make her practice the mind of giving before she passed on to the next life, and that is why he was not going to see his aunt even though she wanted to give him everything. Master Son said to wait and see what would happen. Master Baek, of course, did not talk about any of this, but since Master Son was a living Buddha, she saw through Master Baek's mind.

Like Master Baek's aunt, most of us hoard our wealth all our lives for the "I." And when the moment of our death approaches, when we know that we can no longer take our wealth with us, we have to give our wealth either to "my" children, or to "my" close relative in order to ease the pain of not being able to take our money with us. Such is the greed of people who do not cultivate their minds, and that was why, since she had no children, Master Baek's aunt tried to give her fortune to her closest blood tie.

After a while, the visits from Master Baek's relatives stopped. Since he absolutely refused to receive the money, his aunt gave away all her wealth to her close relatives, distant relatives, acquaintances—even her kitchen maid and her cleaning boys. Eventually there was no more wealth to hand down to Master Baek, and there was no longer any need to send people to him.

One day Master Baek put a huge pile of large bills in a bag and went out to give it all to his aunt. She had been strongly attached to money all her life. Now that she had no money, her mind had become poor, and he wanted to save her from her own poverty-stricken mind. Although his aunt refused to accept the money, he told her to take it and almost forced her to keep it. If you die while imprinting the single notion of "having enough money" in your mind, you will have a lot of money in your next life.

For this reason, people who care for the elderly should always give them enough spending money. When you attend to an elderly person, you should not let him or her imprint the notion of "not having enough money" in his or her mind. Furthermore, if an elderly person is sick, you must do everything to cure his or her disease, for if he or she passes away with the mind-set of being sick, he or she will suffer from disease again in his or her next life.

After a few years, the posallim became curious about what had happened to Master Baek's aunt, so she asked Master Son, "Did his aunt receive a human body?" And Master Son replied, "Of course; his aunt is a seven-year-old boy now, and though he is just a young child, he has a lot of money in his savings account."

An enlightened person uses various methods, depending on one's spiritual advancement or one's use of the mind at each moment, to lead beings to salvation. The enlightened person's measure is not what "I" can get out of it, but how I can make Buddha happy and be beneficial to all beings.

EARNING THREE TIMES YOUR WAGE

E XPRESSING YOUR HEALTHY MIND and body through your work is a joy of life, as refreshing as green grass. Every time you receive a pay-check, try to look back and see whether you have worked with the mind-set of earning three times your wages for the company. If you can do this, you are a wise person, for you only receive the results of the causes that you have planted.

In Korea, I often see that workers at ironworks or people who do odd jobs at construction sites live in a cycle of poverty for their whole life. I wonder if this is because they live lives of incurring debts. For example, often when the workers at ironworks are welding pieces of sheet metal together, they cut up a full sheet when they could easily have used scrap pieces to do the same job. Often they use the resources too wastefully because the materials are not their own.

Some of the roofers I have seen are the same way. As they slate a roof, if the owner of the house did not provide them with generous snacks, they may intentionally make a hole in the roof so that the rain leaks in. I wonder how they are going to cultivate their merit that way. Wouldn't that just increase their karmic debts and cause them to sink further into the cycle of poverty? The rule of causes and conditions is clear.

Many corrupt public officials during the first presidency of Korea also weren't true to their jobs. After they left the public sector, many of them started their own businesses with retirement pensions, but most of them failed. Since they had accumulated so much karmic debt to society while working in the public sector for thirty years, their businesses closed down to fulfill this karmic debt, just as water fills an empty pool. On the other hand, if someone were to diligently plant merit for thirty years, his plant-ed merit would make his business prosperous.

Therefore, one who works with the mentality of earning three times his wages for the company is wise. For example, if you earn five thousand dollars but work with the intention of earning fifteen thousand dollars—five thousand for your employer, five thousand for tax and business expenses, and five thousand for yourself—then you will be successful in your workplace and in any society. Although you would not necessarily work like that, if you have such a mind-set, you would put detailed attention into each job you did, thus becoming more proficient and more productive.

In other words, you should be working with the mentality of an owner. One who has an owner's mentality would only be true to planting merit, whether others appreciate him or not. When you plant your merit in that way, no one but you receives that merit. There is no reason to claim any credit for doing a good job.

WHY MONEY IS NECESSARY

MODERN SOCIETY is based on its economic activities. Thus, one's economic well-being could be compared to the blood circulating in a human body. Just as blood is a basic element in the body, you have to have money to drive cars, buy food, meet people, buy clothes, get a house, get a cup of coffee, and so on. These days, life itself stops if you do not have money. Therefore, financial independence becomes a big part of spiritual independence. When I was studying at Sosa, the fact that we were self-sufficient with the money we earned from our farm helped us to cultivate our confident minds.

It is said that money has its own eyes. In other words, you only earn as much money as you have planted merit. You should plant your merit by saving material goods with a thrifty mentality and by diligently working with the mentality of serving Buddha. Why plant merit?—to provide food, clothes, and a house for the body that is serving Buddha and to use the money in meaningful projects to serve Buddha.

Earning money is important, but spending it is also important. It would be a shame if you spent your money—hard-earned with merit—on seeking pleasure only.

Money is a tool—nothing more and nothing less—that lets people live like human beings. So, isn't it dangerous to think that money is happiness and the answer to your problems? If you always earned and spent your money with a humble mind and with the intention of serving Buddha, the merit vessel that holds your blessed fortune would become bigger and bigger.

There was an owner of a big conglomerate who returned all of his wealth to society before passing away. His son said to him, "Father, please hand down the company to me."

The billionaire, refusing him at once, replied, "I educated you up through college, and you have your own job. Why are you asking for your father's wealth?" The only wealth that he left to his family was a house he had bought for an impoverished nephew.

This billionaire realized the purpose of money and he practiced his own wisdom. Handing down our wealth to our children—because there is no way to take the fortune with us—is the greed of an uncultivated mind. The billionaire, however, started a firm to create jobs for many people in the 1950s, when times were tough. Such a person could be called a living bodhisattva.

According to Buddhism, a world will soon begin where material wealth is abundant, and life is comfortable due to the development of science and technology. This will be the period of "great merit of no limit," the world in which Tathagata Maitreya will appear. We should invoke a wŏn to Buddha, wishing that everyone can be free from poverty and that everyone can have plenty of material wealth, so that they can serve Buddha well.

OFFERING A MEAL TO A DHARMA SEEKER

THERE WAS A TEMPLE called Yŏnhŭng-sa located across from Sosa Monastery. The man who founded the temple was a lay follower named Wŏlgwang. He struggled for a long time in building the temple because he faced many obstacles along the way.

Seeing this, Master Baek told Wŏlgwang that if he fed anyone who entered his house for the next three years, the temple would be built. Just as he was told, after three years of practicing what Master Baek told him, the temple was built.

There is a saying that the merit of serving a meal to one good person is bigger than serving meals to one thousand robbers, and the merit of serving a meal to one spiritual seeker is greater than the merit of serving meals to one thousand good people. It tells us of the rarity of people who cultivate their minds.

Spiritual seekers play the role of incarnations of Buddhas. With bright wŏn and Dharma power, they brighten their surroundings. With their actions and Dharma lectures, they become guides for many people, calming their suffering minds. Because one way of showing reverence to them is materially, offering a meal is an expression of one's mind.

There is a story that explains why Mahakashyapa, one of the Buddha's disciples, was born into a rich family for hundreds of incarnations. Long ago, in one of his past lives, there was a terrible drought. After starving for a couple of days, he was able to get only a bowl of boiled millet. At that time, a pratyeka buddha came to beg for alms.

When Mahakashyapa offered up the bowl of boiled millet to Buddha, the pratyeka buddha gladly enjoyed the meal. Then the pratyeka buddha made a confirmation saying, "Every time you are born, you will become a rich man by this merit," and then he flew away off into the sky. Because of this merit, Mahakashyapa was born into a rich family many times, including during the time of Shakyamuni Buddha.

There is a saying, "Create debts unconditionally to an enlightened person, if it's possible." If you do create such debts, it is said that in whatever incarnation, no matter what hell you fall into, you will be the first to be led to salvation.

OFFERING AND ACCEPTING DEVOTION

EVERY YEAR, when summer came to Sosa, I would cut the grass around the monastery—one cart before noon and one cart after noon—to feed the cows. While I was cutting grass, I was usually able to find places where raspberries grew in abundance. Each time I discovered those fully ripened berries hidden in the forest, near the bank of a small stream, I couldn't have been any happier. By the mysterious stream bank, untouched by people, the luscious berries shone out red under the green bushes. The joy of discovering that delicious sight became even greater in my anticipation of serving them to my teacher.

On rainy days, because we couldn't work in the fields, we had some free time. At such times, I would put on my raincoat and go on an expedition to all the different valleys that I had noticed a couple of days before and fill empty baskets with raspberries. Since I was going to serve the berries to Master Baek, my mind and body were full of joy. It was my simple devotion that wanted to offer up everything to my teacher, who was enlightening my eternity.

Once, after I had been living at Sosa Monastery for four years, I returned home for the first time. After staying at home for about two weeks, I returned to Sosa and stopped by Haein-sa Temple on the way. Since it was autumn, the merchants were selling *tarae* fruit. Hoping to offer them to my master, I bought some and carried them in a paper box. In those days, there were no highways, and after a long drive on unpaved roads, I reached Sosa and opened the box of tarae. Many of the fruits were squashed and looked unappealing. So I told the lady who was in charge of the kitchen that I could not offer the fruits to my teacher in such a condition, and I asked her to just throw them away. But she felt badly about throwing them away and put them on a tray to serve to our teacher. He enjoyed them all. My master had delightedly accepted my devotion, as well as my care in constantly worrying about the fruits being squashed while I was on the bus.

When enlightened people accept your offerings, they are not accepting the material goods, but rather your devotion and care. Master Baek gladly accepted the foods that were offered in reverence and devotion, but he rarely ate food offered otherwise. A poor posallim used to save a little bit of money, taking a few cents from her grocery money each day, and she used it to buy fruit to offer up to Master Baek. The fruit she bought was not very good, but Master Baek enjoyed it all. Perhaps this is why the Buddha is called an *arhat,* or "worthy one," for he is worthy of accepting offerings.

THE MENTALITY OF NOT BEING INDEBTED

WHEN A GAMBLER STARTS with twenty dollars and wins two hundred dollars, he becomes fiercely attached to that extra money as soon as it comes into his hands. So every time he loses some of that money, he becomes heartbroken. Everything except the original twenty dollars is free money, the loss of which should not upset him, yet he feels as if the extra money is the fruit of his honest labor. He thinks that the extra money is his and he laments losing it.

The mentality of seeking rewards without any effort is the nature of ordinary people. We wait for some distinguished man from the east to show up in due time to help us (a Korean expression for waiting for good luck to come by), like a person waiting under a plum tree for a ripe plum to fall into his mouth.

Nothing in the world is free, however. When someone gives something to you for free, he photographs the action of giving deep within his mind. When you receive something for free, you also impress that moment deeply in your mind, and, in your next life, you must pay back whatever you have received.

The mind that likes free things is that of a beggar and is an indebted mind. There is a saying that goes, "Even if you have only a crop of potatoes, if your mind-set is that of serving the potatoes to others, you have a rich person's mind. But, even if you have a crop of rice, which is more highly valued, if you have the mind-set of wanting to be served, you have the beggar's mind."

According to one of the sutras, Queen Mallika's five litter bearers were five monks whom Queen Mallika had served in her past life. It is said that, in order to repay the debt of the offerings that they had accepted from the queen, the monks had to spend their whole life carrying her carriage.

Also, long ago in India, monkeys would sometimes pick fruit and offer it to the ascetics who were devoting themselves to spiritual practice.

As a result of such actions, when the monkeys were reborn as humans, the ascetics who had accepted the fruit were often said to have become their subordinates.

If you become the master of your economic and spiritual life and live with the giving, sharing mind, you can become enlightened.

OFFERING TO BUDDHA WITH REVERENCE WILL
FREE YOUR KARMIC DEBTS

How about invoking a wŏn to Buddha as you are giving or receiving things? "May those who are giving and receiving this object be freed from all the karmic retributions and karmic hindrances they have accumulated for eons. May all families be freed from misfortune, and may their wishes all come true so that they can serve Buddha well, parwŏn!"

If I invoke such a wŏn, and the mind of the person who gives me the object becomes attached to the object, that mind gets offered up to Buddha. I also accumulate merit by offering up the object itself to Buddha. Since I will then be using an object that already has been offered to Buddha, I do not fall into the karma of giving and receiving. Therefore, I don't incur any karmic debt to the giver.

It is said that whenever a bodhisattva wishes to make an offering to Buddha, the offering just springs out of the bodhisattva's palm. Any time the bodhisattva generates a wish, it is realized because the bodhisattva has been making offerings to Buddha for so many lifetimes and has accumulated so much merit.

When you lack certain goods or when you want something, surrender that sense of need or want to Buddha. Offer up anything you obtain to Buddha—whether you have received goods from someone else or have bought them from a store—and then use them for yourself. By surrendering your sense of want or need and by offering up all the things you obtain to Buddha, you accumulate the great merit of no limit that provides you with anything anytime a need arises.

Since the Dharma-body Buddha—the radiance of the Buddha—exists everywhere, any place where you make an offering is the Buddha hall, and any place where you generate reverence to Buddha is the pure land of Buddha, both within and without.

A BOWL OF RICE

IN ORDER FOR A BOWL of rice to get to your table, the heavens must have let the sun shine to grow the rice paddy and scattered just enough rain to wet the shoots. The earth must have opened its heart to let the rice spread its roots, and the wind must have blown cool breezes to ripen the crops. The whole process must be teeming with the sweat of the farmer who planted the rice in spring, pulled the weeds in summer, harvested the crops in fall, and with the care of the one who made the warm bowl of rice, soaking it and boiling it.

Not only that but, in order for today's farming and the table in front of you to exist, there had to be vertical accumulation of technologies from numerous ancestors and traditions. Horizontally there were precious efforts to produce farming tools, fertilizers, threshers, a rice mill, kitchen utensils, fuel, and so on. Therefore, how can you call a bowl of rice yours just because you bought it with your money?

Trace its history—in a bowl of rice, there is the grace of the entire human race and the whole universe. Thus, when you face a bowl of rice, you should first offer it up to Buddha, who is the guiding light of the human race and of nature. Be grateful to the ones who provided the meal, while invoking a wŏn to serve Buddha well. Do this not only with food but also with clothes, books, and shoes. If you offer them all up to Buddha first and then use them, isn't that living in accord with the Dharma?

Six

Reverence, the Fragrance
of Eternity

———

TREES IN FRONT OF THE BUDDHA HALL

WHEN DARK CLOUDS storm in with their harsh rain and wind, all the insects and animals hide in their holes in the ground. Even the leaves curl up. But on a sunny day they all emerge, reaching out to the sun. The sun can be compared to Buddha. Reaching out to the sun may be the sprouting of faith that reaches out for brightness.

Once, I was standing behind the Buddha hall, in a nondual state of mind, completely empty of everything, just looking at the trees. As I watched, I saw the trees standing there with reverence, as if they were bowing their tops slightly toward the Buddha hall. I had just witnessed a split second when even the grass and trees solemnly took refuge in the bright Buddha hall.

NONDUALITY BASED ON
UTMOST REVERENCE

IT IS SAID THAT to be a truly free person you must have the spirit of "Kill the Buddha and kill the patriarchs." My guess, however, is that such a statement is only helpful for those who are at the level of Bodhidharma. In his Dharma lecture, Master Baek once said that, when Bodhidharma was practicing, Buddha's image often appeared in his visions. Bodhidharma tried to break the image with the thought, "Kill the Buddha and kill the patriarchs."

Such ideas can only be uttered at the level of one who is almost a living Buddha—such as Bodhidharma—at his special stage of practice. Wouldn't it be hazardous to advise ordinary people in this way? Bodhidharma must have made the statement in regard to the state of nondiscrimination, wherein one is not even attached to the Buddha. Yet even the state of nondiscrimination—nonduality—should be achieved on the basis of utmost reverence if it is to be enlightening.

Still, you should neither see Buddha as the object of reverence, nor "I" as a separate subject of reverence. In the place of absolute reverence, there is no "I"; therefore, there is nothing to be distinguished. For this reason, Master Baek told us not to picture Buddha as an object of reverence separate from us. Instead, he told us to simply bow to our reverent minds that call out, "Lord Buddha" and to focus our practice toward those reverent minds as if we were to perceive Buddha.

In the mind that is full of ego, a claim that one has reached the nondiscriminative state is merely empty words. It is a karmic hindrance. Since there is no "I" in absolute reverence, however, everything you do with that reverence naturally becomes nondual. Your mind should be one of unconditionally folding your hands and bowing the moment you hear the word "Buddha," so that you can plant merit and become enlightened. Isn't trying to become enlightened "by yourself," without any reverence, just practicing your ego? Trying to become enlightened through your ego is like trying to prepare a bowl of rice with sand.

SURRENDER WITH REVERENCE

IT WAS THE YEAR I turned twenty-eight at Sosa. One day, after finishing the morning practice, I headed back to my room. Remembering that there was something I needed to ask my master, I turned around, and on my way back I perceived an energy that completely filled the sky, incredibly solemn and bright. It was just before dawn.

That fully bright energy was tremendously solemn and heavy. The moment I perceived it, I gasped as though I was being smothered by something, as if the universe were falling on my chest. It was overwhelming. I stared blankly into the sky and probably recited *Mirŭk Chon Yŏrae Pul* in my mind.

Immediately I went to my teacher and asked him about my experience. He explained, "You have just perceived the *Dharmakaya* (Dharmabody Buddha). It shows that the ego has melted away. When this happens, you should fold your hands and bow down halfway saying, 'I will serve you well.' Did you do that?" When I told him that I had not, he told me to do so right away and personally showed me how.

He said that if you do not practice your reverence in ordinary times, you will run into trouble in such a situation. The moment you witness the Dharmakaya, if you generate reverence to the Buddha by saying, "I will serve you well," you will advance even further in your spiritual practice. But if you do not generate reverence, but stand stiff, with the attitude of "I am as much of a Buddha as you are," or with the attitude of "Kill the Buddha, kill the patriarchs," the bright energy of Dharmakaya will strike down your ego. When that happens, you will change your body in three days. For example, there was once a person at Sosa Monastery who perceived the Dharmakaya in his past life while practicing Zen. But he said that, since he did not pay reverence to the Dharmakaya, he was punished by it.

Each time your discriminating mind calms, you witness radiance.

This means that you are perceiving the Buddha, for there isn't anywhere on earth where Tathagata Maitreya has not cultivated his virtues. He remains as white radiance all over the universe.

However, you should not keep such concepts as "Dharmakaya" or "radiance" in your mind. Even Buddha is no longer "Buddha" when you enclose him in your mind—Buddha becomes only your mind's discriminative notion.

There once was an accomplished master who had never met a fully enlightened one, so he always held a preconceived notion of Buddha as bright radiance. He lived his whole life with that preconceived notion, unable to surrender it. When Master Baek searched for that monk with his wisdom-eye after he had passed away to see where he went, Master Baek found him trapped in light that looked like white pottery. Since the monk pictured Buddha as radiance in his mind and directed his mind toward it, he could only end up sitting inside a luminous and cloudy light. Master Baek broke the pottery of light and guided him to salvation.

As this master's fate illustrates, it becomes a problem if you draw anything in your mind. You should surrender even the discriminative notion of who Buddha is and surrender the act of surrendering. No matter what type of discriminating mind it is, you should surrender it in that short moment of nonduality and nonwandering thoughts, when you call out with all your heart and with reverence, "Buddha!"

KING ASHOKA

THE FOLLOWING EVENTS took place while Buddha was residing in Jeta Grove, the garden of Anathapindika's park in Shravasti. One day, as usual, Buddha entered the city of Shravasti to collect alms with Ananda. They encountered some children on the road, playing happily with mud. They pretended that it was treasure or food and piled it up in a mud storehouse.

One of the children saw the Buddha coming his way from afar. He was filled with joy at Buddha's holy appearance, so he wanted to make an offering to Buddha. But there was nothing to offer him besides the mud treasures and mud crops.

Since he was too tiny, he asked another child to let him climb up on his back. He offered up one fistful of mud crops from the mud storehouse to the Buddha. Seeing the child's devotion and kindness, the Buddha lowered his bowl to receive the offering. The Buddha gave the mud to Ananda, saying, "Plaster my room with this mud."

After they had returned to the temple, Ananda plastered a corner of Buddha's room with the mud. It disappeared quickly for it was such a small amount. Ananda told the Buddha, "I plastered a corner of your room with the child's mud, Lord." Buddha, with a joyous look, gave this Dharma lecture to Ananda:

"Ananda, that child has offered a fistful of mud with reverence to Buddha, and covered a corner of my room with it. From this merit, in his next life, he will become the king of a great nation, and he will be called Ashoka.

"The children who were playing with him will become his ministers and rule the nation together. They will uphold the three jewels of Buddha, Dharma, and Sangha, make offerings to many, spread Buddha's relics everywhere, and build eighty-four thousand stupas to greatly propagate the Buddhadharma."

VENERABLE SHARIPUTRA

ONCE, WHEN THE BUDDHA was first spreading the Dharma, one of his monks was walking down the street, exuding his Dharma power. Just then, Shariputra was passing by that area, and he was greatly impressed by the way the monk carried himself. So Shariputra went up to him and asked, "Who is your teacher?"

The monk replied, "My teacher is Gautama Siddhartha."

Shariputra asked again, "What is his teaching?"

"He teaches that everything arises from causes and conditions, and everything ceases when the causes and conditions cease."

On hearing such an enlightening Dharma lecture for the first time, a great admiration for Shakyamuni Buddha arose in Shariputra's mind. So, he asked the monk to lead him to the Buddha, and taking his friend Maudgalyayana with him, they immediately joined the Buddhist order.

From then on, the Venerable Shariputra always paid reverence to the monk who introduced him to the Buddha. Because that monk was practicing in the East, the Venerable Shariputra never slept with his feet in that direction. If his reverence to the one who introduced him to Buddha is that great, how great must be his devotion to his teacher?

SNOW AND STAR

ONCE I CULTIVATED a desolate mountain slope at Sosa. Besides the approximately three acres of land that we farmed, we also cultivated about three acres on a mountain face to create a pasture for cows.

Normally, due to our busy schedule, I would not have even dreamt of pursuing such a venture, but I started the project in winter, when I still had some free time. I put the rocks that were scattered all over the mountains and fields in my rack and placed them in the troughs between the planted pastures. Despite the freezing weather that had dropped the mercury to fifteen degrees below zero, and even in the middle of a blizzard, I made spare time to clear the mountain by myself.

As I was working, I surrendered all sorts of mental obstacles—such as cold weather, wind, and snow—with a loud recitation of *Mirŭk Chon Yŏrae Pul.* When at last my practice seemed to be continuing smoothly, I saw my aged master in the distance walking up through snow falling so heavy that it almost blocked one's vision. He had come all the way up there for the chance to strengthen my practice of surrendering. When an enlightened master gives such a confirmation at the moment Dharma awakens in you, your practice becomes stronger.

I could only be grateful to him. Overwhelmed with deference, I wasn't even able to greet him properly. I just worked with the rack on my back while continuing my practice. He silently looked at me awhile, then, after invoking a wŏn for me, he slowly walked back down the hill. Seeing him carefully walk down the snowy hill, I folded my hands and bowed while invoking a wŏn, "May I be able to attend our teacher well, so I can serve Buddha well."

One day, when Sosa was entirely white with snow, I came down from my room around two in the morning to clear a path. I was worried that our teacher might slip while he was going to the bathroom. Unbeknownst to me, my master had already come outside, aware that I was hard at work clearing away the snow.

While standing there, he gave an incredible Dharma lecture on the mysterious realm of enlightenment until 4:30 in the morning. The moment I heard my master's own voice telling me about the mysterious, secretive realm of Buddha, and his own experiences with things that one can hardly even imagine, my reverence and wŏn of admiration toward Buddha blossomed more greatly and clearly than the white glimmer of the snow, the pure vitality of daybreak, or the early morning sky.

As the Dharma lecture was about to end, bright stars sparkled in the blue sky of dawn.

VISITING THE MASTER AT DAYBREAK

WHEN I WAS RUNNING A BUSINESS, I would take the first bus once a week from the Seoul train station to Inch'ŏn at 4:10 A.M. to visit my master at Sosa and to practice there. Those times, reverently beholding his compassion and listening to his Dharma lecture, my heart was filled with awe and radiance.

My memory of visiting him on one cold winter day is especially vivid, and I am transported once more back to that time:

It is the day before I am supposed to go to Sosa. I go to the grocery store, and I pick the best and the freshest fruits to offer my teacher. When I wipe the fruits with cautious hands, three times each with a wet towel and a dry towel in order not to bruise them, the fragrance of reverence and joy, thicker than that of the fruit, seems to permeate the entire town.

In the middle of my reciting the sutra, the siren sounds at 4:00 A.M. to end the curfew. As I go to his place with the fruit under my coat and suit, embracing them with my body heat, since they might freeze in the cold weather of minus ten degrees, my mind is that of a seeker whose whole life is surrendered to Buddha and to my master.

As I walk the streets with a cool head and a warm heart, the hazy white radiance, as peaceful as the fog of early morning, seeps into every corner of my tranquil mind. This bright mind, free of its body, is headed only to the enlightened master, to the place of refuge. The wŏn, made before Buddha, of a wayfarer who is awakened to the importance of his master must have been realized.

I have been Master Baek's student since the time of Shakyamuni Buddha. I have been his student since long before Shakyamuni Buddha's time to the time he was in Jerusalem, in the Middle East, in China, and at Kŭmgang Mountain. Having been awakened to his Dharma lamp for so long, how can I not revere him?

The first bus arrives at the corner of Sosa in no time. When I get off the bus, the light from the distant white cross on the top of Shinangch'on comes into sight, and the cold morning air seeps into my body.

As I picture myself reflecting on the wisdom of an enlightened master, I hurry to his place. The karmic hindrances that I have surrendered well, thus strengthening my practice, and the karmic hindrances that have escaped from me all come to my mind clearly. As I reflect on those moments, my tense mind surrenders them even harder by reciting *Mirŭk Chon Yŏrae Pul.*

When I arrive in front of the gate, where a carving of the Diamond Sutra passage "Thus ye shall view" hangs, the master is already waiting for me, as if he knew I was coming.

"You're here! The door lock is frozen from the snow. I'll bring some hot water." My teacher's voice is as rich as a thick iron chain being dragged across a cement floor.

He brings some hot water with a dipper to melt the ice and to open the door for me. Under his warm winter hat, a look of delight settles on his radiant face, a look full of compassion. He is wearing a thick winter jacket, gray wool pants, and shoes lined with artificial fur.

After passing through the long white corridor, I enter the Buddha hall. There is bright energy all around, brighter than the fluorescent light reflected by the white walls of the Buddha hall. The warmth of the room thaws my freezing hands and cheeks.

My teacher enters through the back corridor, and after giving me a cushion to sit on, he sits on a cushion with a pleased look on his face. When I bow down to him three times, he invokes a wŏn for me. With the sound of his energetic Dharma voice, the past week's pain and suffering melts away, and strength surges through my body.

When he tells me to practice surrendering while kneeling but keeping my hips and back straight and goes into the next room, I place my cushion about thirty centimeters away from the wall and start reciting *Mirŭk Chon Yŏrae Pul.* I practice surrendering while gazing at the wall.

My wish to be with him and listen to him speak is even greater than my wish to practice. So when I see him going to the next room, I am a bit disappointed. Being aware of my mind, he says, "Well, then," and sits down again to give me a Dharma lecture.

Twenty minutes into the practice, the pores on my back start stinging. A little longer into the practice, the palms of my folded hands and my back start becoming warm, and soon my whole body is sweating. At that moment, my body and mind couldn't possibly have felt any better. After I sweat, my master finally comes out and tells me to sit down, and I finish my practice.

Sometimes, on the bare floor, I practice surrendering for about four hours in this kneeling position, but he still does not come out of his room. At such times, my body becomes soaked with sweat. Also, since I have been practicing with a loud recitation, my voice is strained and hoarse for about three of those four hours. But when I continue my practice, my voice suddenly bursts open and becomes even clearer than before. My whole body is tired, and my knees are numb, beyond the point of sensing any pain, but my body and mind are refreshed. I feel as if I could fly away.

During practice, all the memories of recent painful or regrettable incidents come to my mind. I feel exactly the way I felt when those incidents happened. This sickens my heart and clouds my mind. As the practice goes on, those painful feelings become thinner and lose their color until my mind becomes light and calm.

Gradually, as the remaining heavy feelings that have not yet been surrendered are finally surrendered, my heart calms and my mind is focused. At that point, I am in a natural state of no thought, no action. In that state, if I want to know the answer to a question, I recite *Miruk Chon Yorae Pul* to that question and an answer comes to me. Sometimes, if my practice of surrendering continues well, I even perceive the white radiance.

When my master comes back, I end my practice and ask him the questions that occurred to me during practice. He explains them to me one by one. If there are things that I can't understand, he tells me to constantly surrender that sense of not being able to understand.

He then gives a Dharma lecture for many hours. The realm of his Dharma lecture is simply bright. Master Baek, with his Buddha-eye, has an awareness that penetrates through the past, present, and future of all things and beyond. He lectures about the physical attributes of people who attended Shakyamuni Buddha, the Dharma lectures of the Buddha, the depth and shape of certain valleys of the Kun Lun Mountain, and the plants that live within that valley. He lectures as if he is actually there. He also lectures on the law behind the creation of the universe, the destiny of nations and the world, and deep questions of physics. When he is asked about any person, he knows his or her face, mind, and future in detail.

His is the mind that knows everything due to surrendering all the things he doesn't know. Though he has never read about them or heard about them, he just knows them. I am simply amazed at how he knows everything. Each time I come to study with him, he lectures on something new. He does not teach us from his memory. Depending on the people he teaches, he uses the most adequate answers to suit each person. No matter how unfamiliar our questions are, there is no question that he does not answer from his bright mirror of wisdom. He knows everything by surrendering the discriminative notion of not knowing.

Since my mind is reverently directed to him as I hear his Dharma lecture, I receive his radiance in full. After meeting with him, the energy I receive from him lasts for a whole week.

Around 10 A.M. we have breakfast at the same table. Sometimes there is no one working in the kitchen and he says, "I'll get the breakfast ready. You just continue your practice here." Out of deference, I reply, "I'll get the breakfast ready, Sir."

Then he says, "No, it's okay. Since you're unfamiliar with the kitchen, I'll go prepare the meal."

It is a simple menu. Whenever he eats *kimch'i,* he starts eating from the outer, blue part of the cabbage that has already lost its taste. In the tranquillity of the meal, there is only the occasional sound of spoons clanking. It is a moment when even the sense of taste has been surrendered, so we finish the meal without any notion of taste. We are simply full.

Around noon, I say, "Master, since the briquette fire is nearly out, I have to go back to the store now."

When I get up to leave, he says, "Here, take the lit briquette with you," and laughs cheerfully. He tells me to practice surrendering continually. After I give him three bows and leave, he comes out to the door as usual to see me off with his carefree laughter, like that of a loving grandfather.

WHEN YOU GIVE THE DIAMOND SUTRA

YOU SHOULD ONLY GIVE the Diamond Sutra to someone who will definitely read it, for if the person who receives the sutra despises it or steps on it, that person will get stepped on by someone else. And when that happens, the person will then try to get his revenge on the one who gave him the sutra. Therefore, how can we not be careful?

Once, I gave copies of the Diamond Sutra to my nephews, who believed in a different religion. These children, who were in high school and middle school, could not have known the importance of the sutra. I gave them the sutras only because I wished to do so.

Later, by chance, I told Master Baek what I had done. He said that they would trample on my head. I asked him why, and he said that they would receive karmic retribution for belittling the sutra, and, since my nephews would receive this retribution because of me, they would step on my head. He said that when you give a sutra to someone get two or three confirmations that they will read it and give it only to a person who asks for it.

Once, I also left about four hundred midsized Diamond Sutras at a follower's home. I had been worried that I had no place to enshrine the sutras, so she suggested enshrining them at her house. A couple of days after I had enshrined them, a mischievous boy of that household exchanged them for candy at a junkshop. When I found this out, I was so shocked that I almost fainted.

Even after searching all the junkshops in P'ohang, Taegu, and Pusan, I could not find the sutras. I searched the shops in P'ohang again carefully and found three bundles of one hundred each. But still I could not find the remaining bundle. A few days later, the boy who had sold the sutras was in a train accident. It was summertime, and he was sleeping on top of the railroad tracks when a train ran him over. He was hurt badly, but his limbs were not cut off. It was the worst experience.

I told my master about the incident and was scolded by him again.

In the *Sutra of Karmic Causality*, there is a verse about a person becoming a hunchback due to the karmic retribution of throwing the sutra on the ground. Also, in the Diamond Sutra, it is written that if you enshrine the Diamond Sutra and study it well, Buddha sees this, and the bright force that surrounds the area will protect the place where the Diamond Sutra is enshrined.

The Diamond Sutra is the sutra that contains Buddha's mind. It is a precious teacher that makes us reach toward Buddha's enlightenment and helps us to learn and practice that enlightenment. Aside from worrying about karmic retribution, if we simply enshrine the sutra well and give it to others wisely, we will develop the proper attitude of one who studies Buddhadharma.

Seven

May We All Serve Buddha Well,

Parwŏn!

———

MAY WE ALL SERVE
BUDDHA WELL, PARWŎN!

ORDINARILY, WE MAKE OFFERINGS to Buddha and pray for ourselves and for the health of our family, happiness, academic achievements, success in business, and cures from illnesses. I suppose if you prayed fervently enough, these wishes could come true for you. But, from a spiritual practitioner's point of view, such prayers can become a problem because, if you keep practicing the mentality of begging from Buddha, you may very well end up weakening yourself. The more you beg from Buddha, the more your mind becomes that of a beggar; the more you depend on Buddha, the weaker your mind becomes.

There is a difference, for example, between saying, "Buddha, please make so and so pass the entrance exam" and saying, "May so and so pass the entrance exam so that he can serve Buddha well, parwŏn!" Though the content is the same, the prayers differ both in their intentions and in their results.

The first prayer bears the mentality of hoping to obtain what one wants from Buddha. Such an attitude can turn into resentment of the Buddha if one's wish doesn't come true. But the latter mentality is one of wishing for something in order to serve Buddha well. Such a mindset is righteous and brave. Such a wish becomes the Buddha work that accumulates merit before the Buddha.

More aggressively, one can invoke wŏns such as, "Lord Buddha, may I surrender all my arising minds and eternally enlighten this one mind, so that I can make Buddha happy, parwŏn!" or, "I do not have the ability to make Buddha happy right now, but with diligent effort, I vow to make Buddha happy, parwŏn!" or, "By helping to spread Buddha's bright Dharma to many people, may I serve Buddha well, parwŏn!" The person who invokes these wŏns practices a brave and enlightened mind.

Since the proper mentality is to serve the omnipotent Buddha—who completely fills the universe—with this mind, how brave and grand the basis for such an intention is! By performing such virtuous deeds, one accumulates merit in one's mind and awakens wisdom. When one attains the ability to serve and support even the universe with one's mind, one has undoubtedly achieved Buddhahood. Therefore, the brightest and greatest wŏn that we can make is the wŏn to serve Buddha well. Becoming one with this wŏn and always serving Buddha is the great path that leads to enlightenment.

Let's continually invoke wŏns. For everyone you run into, invoke a wŏn. "May this person awaken faith and devotion so that he or she can serve Buddha well, parwŏn!" For every incident you face, "May this thing be resolved brightly to serve Buddha well, parwŏn!" For every thought that arises, "May this thought be surrendered well to serve Buddha well, parwŏn!" "May bright wisdom arise to serve Buddha well, parwŏn!" Even when looking at the sky and the trees, pray, "May nature awaken faith and devotion in me to serve Buddha well, parwŏn!"

BUDDHA WORK IS BASED ON WŎN

GOALS SHOULD BE PURSUED with a natural flow instead of an artificial force. The basis for such a flow is the power that comes from making persistent wŏns. If you pursue a goal and become involved before the time and atmosphere are ripe, you will clash with the existing atmosphere and create discord and dissonance. On the other hand, if you constantly invoke wŏns and the power of your wŏn is ripe, you will see that the atmosphere becomes bright and the goal is accomplished naturally.

If you say, "I'll do it in such and such a way," then the action is directed at and concluded in you. But if you say, "May it be done in such and such a way to serve Buddha well, parwŏn!" then your action is directed instead toward the radiance of the Buddha. In everything you do, you'll plant merit before Buddha, and the work will end up being the Buddha's work.

Thus Master Baek always lectured, "Do not say, 'I will do something,' but instead invoke a wŏn before Buddha. Then you will be free from your ego of 'I,' and your work will become part of the greater flow of Buddha work." Master Baek told us to invoke a wŏn for everything we do.

GREAT WŎN CAN MOVE THE UNIVERSE

SINCE THE ENTIRE UNIVERSE is believed to have arisen from the minds of sentient beings, is there anything that we cannot achieve through the power of a wŏn of wishing to serve Buddha well? It is said that a single mind's wŏn can move the universe. There are certain times when things cannot be achieved, due to a lack of merit. But if your wŏn is powerful enough, your goal can be achieved, regardless of your level of merit.

Once, when I was at Sosa, we were short on workers. So, I began to hope that a good worker would enter our monastery, and soon such a person came. I had some free time, so when I wished to spend it studying Buddhism academically, a graduate of Dongguk University with a degree in Buddhism came to the monastery. Even in a monastery, the comings and goings of people happen according to one's wŏn.

Yesterday, I read a newspaper article saying that the students from P'ohang University of Science and Technology all study textbooks written in foreign languages. They are so advanced that they finish in two weeks a computer program that would take about six months for three professionals to complete. They are an amazingly talented group, and one wonders how a school with such students could be established in a tiny city like P'ohang.

Five or six years before P'ohang University of Science and Technology was built, our teacher said that, since someone had a great wŏn to produce talented people, there was going to be a world-class institution built in his home town. He also said that many huge conglomerates had been built on the strength of one or two of their founders' wŏn and merit. He said that a few people with great wŏns and merit can move the world, and furthermore, in some cases, a single person's strength of wŏn can move the entire universe.

When you look at the world today, you see many problems, like disease, hunger, war, political and economic discord, and so on. From an individual's point of view, misfortunes such as disease are said to be karmic hindrances carried over from a past incarnation. However, if many people invoke bright wŏns, the force of their wŏns combined can eradicate such misfortunes and benefit many people.

My teacher has said that, before the era of Maitreya Buddha comes, there will be five disasters: death through flooding, through fire, through starvation, through war, and through disease. These events will come about as a process of purifying and neutralizing the negative karmas we have accumulated over successive past incarnations. While these disasters are going on, there will be clashes between the world's religions. Once the religious discord ceases, eternal peace will reign, and a paradise will be established on earth. Countries will function in peace and harmony, and the world's nations will trade with one another.

Those serving Buddha are the people who invoke wŏns to solve the real problems of today. They invoke the wŏns that prepare the way for this bright future.

EVERY MOMENT WE FULFILL OUR WISH,
YET EVERY MOMENT WE COMPLAIN

A CERTAIN POSALLIM made a wŏn saying she wanted nothing except an intelligent and good-natured son-in-law. Because she had been practicing devoutly for three years, her wish came true, and she married off her daughter.

As it happened, her new son-in-law had also been invoking a wŏn to marry the daughter of a wealthy family, a family that was also devoutly Buddhist. The bride's household was one of the wealthiest in the city, and the young man's family was so poor that they did not even own a television set. Nonetheless, he had paid his way through Seoul National University's Law School, and he was studying for his bar exam. Since the bride's mother had to convince her husband to permit the marriage, she lied to him, saying that the young man's family was well off while secretly paying the groom's wedding expenses herself. For three years now, she has been providing their living expenses while her son-in-law studies for his bar exam.

One day, she came to me and complained about her lot, saying that she didn't know why she had to face such trouble. People fulfill their wishes every second of their lives, and they complain every second of their lives. When she was invoking the wŏn, if she had said, "a son-in-law who is well off and also intelligent" instead of saying, "nothing except," the situation would have been completely different. She invoked such a wŏn because she was unwise. Her wŏn came true, but she still complained.

One should always invoke a bright wŏn, a complete wŏn, the result of which is "to serve Buddha well, parwŏn!" This way it becomes Buddha work and one plants merit through it. But because people are not able to do that, they complain.

THE GOVERNOR OF KYŎNGSANG PROVINCE

DURING THE YI DYNASTY in Korea, the governor of Kyŏngsang Province had his office in Andong. In a town in Andong, there lived a young couple and their six-year-old boy. On the day that the governor of Kyŏngsang Province was to arrive for his post, the town held a festive procession with much fanfare, and when the six-year-old boy saw the procession, he said to his father:

"Dad, when I grow up, I am going to become the governor of Kyŏngsang Province, too."

And his father said, "You cannot become a government official because you are a person of low birth."

On hearing this, the child was shocked. He began to wither and weaken, and eventually he passed away. The father was so shattered that every year he made an offering for his son on the anniversary of the night he died.

Fourteen years later, a twelve-year-old governor of Kyŏngsang Province came to office. While touring many different places in Andong, she found a familiar town.

For many years, on the seventh day of every eleventh lunar month, she had dreamed of a small stream that flowed through a thick, old pine forest. Past the stone bridge by the stream, there was a thatched house just outside the town, and inside the brushwood gate, there were two Chinese date trees standing in front of the well near the house. In her dream, she used to open the brushwood gate and go into the house, where she was served a great deal of food. She had had that exact dream the day before, and now she stood in that very town.

She opened the brushwood gate of the house with the two Chinese date trees standing in front of the well. A man who seemed to be slightly less than forty years old came out of the room and saw the governor. Next, a lady came out of the kitchen, having heard someone open the brushwood gate.

The twelve-year-old governor of Kyŏngsang spoke first. "Was there an offering in this house last night, by any chance?"

The couple looked at each other in surprise. The husband answered, "Yes! There was an offering here last night. But how did you know that?"

"Last night, I dreamed of coming here and eating a lot of food. But who is the offering for?"

The man replied, "It was an offering for our son, but…"

The governor asked, "Why were you making an offering for your son?"

Since the young governor was curious, they told her the full story of their son, who had died fourteen years before. While listening to the story, the governor's heart overflowed with emotion. She held their hands tightly and said, "You must be the father and mother of my past life." With that, the governor crumpled on the spot and died without a word.

Fourteen years before, the six-year-old child was shocked and had died with a wish unfulfilled. The spirit was born in the body of a princess in order to become the governor of Kyŏngsang. At age twelve, she had begged the king, her maternal grandfather, to let her become the governor. As soon as she had fulfilled her wish, she changed her body and passed away just like that.

SENTIENT BEINGS LEAVE THE WORLD
AFTER FULFILLING THEIR WISHES

SOMETIMES, WHEN PEOPLE finally gain wealth and begin to enjoy themselves after having led a poverty-stricken life, they pass away. Their relatives lament, for the deceased did not even get to enjoy life once it finally turned around for them. Because such a person's sole wish is to become wealthy, when that wish finally ripens and he is actually able to live well, his mind wears out completely and he dies. It is the same as becoming totally exhausted and not being able to get up after finishing an important, anticipated event.

There was a student who, after ten years of hard work to receive his Ph.D., died in a German airport on his way back to Korea. His sole wish was to earn the Ph.D. degree, but when he finally received the degree, he felt, "Did I go through all that just to receive this piece of paper?" The sense of futility made him let go of his mind, and he died.

There is, however, a way to live longer in such situations. If you make such wŏns as "May I be freed from poverty to serve Buddha well, parwŏn!" or "May I receive a Ph.D. to serve Buddha well, parwŏn!" in ordinary times, you will live well in order to serve Buddha. And from that merit of serving Buddha, your life will be even better than what you hoped for. It is because people have no other wish than to be well off or to receive a Ph.D. that they just end with the fulfillment of their wish.

If you do not know how to invoke a wŏn, after you fulfill your wish, you should produce the mentality to do more meaningful things through the wish that has been realized. Leaving the world after fulfilling one's wish is the way of all sentient beings. One who leaves the world after having served Buddha well is fortunate.

TO DEVOTE ONESELF
TO SPIRITUAL PRACTICE

THERE WAS A PERSON who developed tuberculosis at age sixteen, and was bedridden for the next twenty years. Because his mind was weakened from the single notion of being sick, he was always weak even after he was cured.

This man had been a spiritual seeker in his past life, and right before he died, he had invoked a wŏn, "May I receive a human body to continue my practice," and then changed his body. Because of his past wŏn, he got to fully live the life of a spiritual seeker in this incarnation, for the life of a spiritual seeker has so many restrictions—so many things that one cannot do, so many places where one cannot go—that only a bedridden person can fulfill such a life. Thus he lived his entire life as a patient, fulfilling his wish.

For people who are cultivating their minds, the mentality of serving Buddha is more important than their desire to devote themselves to the spiritual practice. If this person had made a wŏn of "May I receive a human body to serve Buddha well, parwŏn!" then he could have served Buddha freely, with a healthy mind and body.

Eight

Absolute Freedom

Is Loneliness

———

ABSOLUTE FREEDOM IS LONELINESS

L ET'S SAY SOMEONE is on a ship, with plenty of food, drifting in the
middle of an ocean by himself. Since there is no one he has to deal
with, all is peaceful for a while. But the depth of loneliness arising from
within becomes too deep and dark for him to climb out. It is as painful
as death itself, for his inner world, filled with loneliness, is withering
away. Human beings are social animals that cannot live alone. Thus, the
loneliness of drifting alone in the middle of an ocean is horrible mental
torture. We can see why serious criminals are put in solitary cells—such
treatment is mental abuse that leaves no physical scar.

Loneliness is the biggest problem that every living being has to solve.
The biggest burden for people who cultivate their minds is freeing themselves from loneliness. If you are busy, your mind is absorbed in your
work and does not have time to become lonely. If you were a traveler,
however, eternally walking alone in a desert, how desperate you would
be for people and conversation! Even our attachment to eating is less
difficult to overcome than loneliness.

A human being might be seen as a single fir tree under a sky of loneliness, reverently folding its hands to the sun from time to time, while
being rained on by the shower of ignorance. With its branches boldly
stretched toward the sun, with its sturdy roots that do not shake in the
wind, it gratefully seeks the rays of sun that shine down on it. It is like
the spiritual seeker looking up to the unknown state called Buddhahood.

Devoting yourself to spiritual practice means picking out and cleaning the seed that is covered with the shade of loneliness and darkness.
The pain of purifying loneliness and the bliss of being freed from it are
special states understood only by those who have cleansed loneliness
from their minds. If one is lonely neither in a crowd nor in the deep
mountains, one is an able person who knows how to enjoy absolute freedom. Such a person could well be a Buddha.

WHEN YOU ARE FREED
FROM LONELINESS

WHEN I FIRST ENTERED Sosa, I was often all by myself in the huge monastery. The other practitioners had not yet come, and my mind was full of loneliness.

During that time, one of the things Master Baek repeatedly told me was a story about his days in public service. When he went to department stores, the salespeople would say, "Sir, you must have many grandchildren, right?" and they would recommend that he buy things for his grandchildren. He said that he appeared to have many grandchildren because he did not feel any loneliness and did not give out any sense of loneliness. He often said that one's spiritual practice is complete when one finishes purifying all the loneliness from one's mind. Because I was only twenty-six-years old, and because I had just started my practice, such lectures did not make much sense to me. I wondered why he told me these stories so often.

Once, he told me to smell myself to see if I could smell any odor of sexual desire on me. He said that people who are freed from all the emotions of male-female relationships, including sexual desire, do not emit any odor from their bodies. People who are liberated from such desires give out a fragrant scent.

Much of literature, music, and art deals with the subject of loneliness. Loneliness is rooted in the desires of the flesh, the attachment to one's body. The creative work of one who has not cleansed his or her desires of the flesh is usually mixed with greed, anger, and arrogance. However, when Buddha is present within one's mind there is no loneliness. One who has purified the root of loneliness does not suffer from being alone.

Master Baek said that in the music of Handel and Bach, for example, there are no desires of the flesh. This is probably because their music has a brightness that reveres the glory of God—the music comes from an attitude of worship and devotion. The words to popular songs are often about unfulfilled love, longing, loneliness, and resentment. Loneliness, a desire of the flesh, is what all living beings must surrender to their very roots, until they finally attain Buddhahood.

KEEP A DISTANCE THE LENGTH
OF A BULL'S REIN WHEN YOU
GET TO KNOW SOMEONE

IF YOU GO TOO NEAR A BULL, you can either be hurt by the bull's sharp horns or receive a friendly gesture and be slobbered on by his wet tongue. On the other hand, if you stand too far away, you'll lose your grip on the rein, and he will run away. A runaway bull ruins vegetable fields, and when you try to catch him, he always runs out of reach when you approach. Thus, the length of a bull's rein is the perfect distance within which to control the bull.

Getting acquainted with people is the same way. If you become too close to someone without having freed yourself from your ego, you will find the other's flaws first. Without realizing that the flaws that you see in the other person are flaws in your mind, you criticize the other person. The other person is the same way. He or she judges you with his or her own flaws.

There is a saying, "When kids become too close to each other, tears come out of their eyes." When you are too close to someone without the ability to control your mind, since your mind is full of ego, your relationship will be unstable. For example, when you like someone, you want to give that person everything you have, even your own flesh, but if you suddenly come to dislike the person, the poison of murderous hatred rises up in you. In the name of friendship, we practice a solicitous mentality, yet ask for things in return for our friendship.

In this way, the darkest spot is right under the lamp. If you're too close to someone, you can't see his virtues. Likewise, if you are too far from him, you cannot see either his virtues or his limitations. One who cultivates the mind should be able to see neither the virtue nor the limitations of others. He or she should see others as Buddhas.

WARMTH IS WITHIN BUDDHA'S BOSOM

WHEN CHILDREN REACH ADOLESCENCE, they start disobeying and rebelling against their parents. This is painful, especially for the mother, because her children defy her after she has nurtured them with all her mind and body. From the children's point of view, however, it is perfectly justified. When they were young they could not survive without their parents, so they had to obey them. Now that they are older, they awaken to the instinct that tells them that they do not need their parents anymore.

At this point, a wise person would say, "I guess this is a sign that they have grown up." He or she would not be disappointed. But parents usually say, "How could they do this to me after all I have done for them?" and demand recognition for their efforts. This is painful for everyone.

Once, an enlightened master went to a cremation site. He saw two children, a nine year old and a ten year old, crying their hearts out after having cremated their mother. When the master looked into their minds, he saw that they were thinking, "How are we going to survive now?" Rather than crying out of sorrow or love for their mother, they were crying because they felt hopeless about their own future. Most people consider their own needs first in this way. When you look at such incidents as parents and children suing each other and killing each other for money, siblings fighting with each other, husbands and wives becoming enemies after a divorce, and close friends not speaking to each other because of their conflicting interests, relationships between human beings seem so heartless. This is because everyone tries to live only for himself or herself.

Most of us fiercely feed our egos by putting "me" before my parents, "me" before my siblings, "me" before my wife, "my interest" before that of the neighbors and the country. This is the innate nature of all beings, for which we can't be blamed.

Whom can we trust and on whom can we depend? If two porcupines were to hug each other out of love, they would pierce each other with their spines. Likewise, we should understand that relationships between beings who still have an ego are usually like porcupines hugging one another. Therefore, we might as well condition our minds to be broad and generous, so that we can hug the people who hurt us. We should condition our minds to be healthy, so that even if we are disturbed by such shocks as betrayal, we can overcome the pain.

The Diamond Sutra states, "all conditioned things are like a dream, a dew drop, a masquerade, or a bubble." Our world is this way and so too are our lives. One should not lose one's mind to a person or to work. Only while looking up to Buddha should we surrender our rising thoughts and emotions, moment after moment.

AN EMBROIDERED PHOENIX MIGHT
BE SEEN, BUT THE NEEDLE TIP
CANNOT BE SEEN

THERE IS A SAYING, "An embroidered phoenix can be seen, but the tip of the needle that created the phoenix cannot be seen." How many tiresome days must someone have worked with that weary needle! We might call this the beautiful virtue that does not display the hardship of blood and tears, but only shows the grandeur of the phoenix to others.

As the saying goes, hiding your hardships in order not to worry others is the practice of a bodhisattva. To the people who have been battered by the rough and tumble of life, we who cultivate our minds shouldn't add any more to their suffering. We should always practice compassion, always try to serve nectar from the sweet spring of life to those with much pain in their minds.

THE ZELKOVA TREE

A PICNIC CROWD rests briefly under the zelkova tree in the park and then leaves. The neighboring town's children take over the vacated tree shade, cooling down the heat of their raucous play, and then leave for the mountain streams to splash in the water. As midday passes, a few of the town's elders gather under the tree to talk about passing affairs of the world and then leave one by one as night approaches.

In the empty park where the sun has set, little mice make their appearance. After running around for the cookie crumbs that were spilled by the visitors, they look for their homes. As the night deepens, a full moon floating in the sky illustrates the evanescence of the world.

The shaded ground under the zelkova tree is a place of excitement and anticipation for the picnicking crowd searching for the mystery of nature, a playground mixed with joy and innocence for youths, a place of the sorrow of alienation and regrets about life for the town's elders, and a place of competition over food for the mice.

All the world's a stage, as Shakespeare once said. The actors, who play their parts and exit, are destined to pass this place again. Meanwhile, it is the tree's habit to carefully record all the actors' stories, both happy and sad, in its two hundred growth rings.

The blue, porcelain sky abruptly enters my vision as I raise my eyes. The cool, blue sea spreads far away and thick forests mysteriously cut across the mountain tops. Even the wide open field—this beautiful land—must be a stage on which we stay briefly and eventually leave behind. The family that we love, the friends whom we love, the nation that we love—when their time is over, the cause and condition, the karmic ties, cease. Thus all will scatter to each of their paths like a flock of sparrows in the morning sky.

Who wrote this play in which we have to laugh, cry, and exit according to the script? No God can write it, nor can Buddha. Only your own mind can write it.

THE VIRTUE OF WATER

WATER IS THE SOURCE of all life. Living one's life like the flow of water means practicing the truth, the Dharma. If there is a rock, water does not fight to go through it but goes around it. If it goes under a rectangular bridge, it takes the shape of the bridge; if it goes through a round pipe, it takes a round shape. Neither does water cling to its color. Instead it washes all things to make them clean. For water does not have the stubbornness of "I"—it is in the state of "no mind."

People always try to put themselves higher, but the water always finds the lowest place. The stream lowers itself to become a river, and the river lowers itself even further until it cannot go any lower and reaches the sea.

When people listen to the murmuring of a stream, it puts them at ease. Water does not compete to go ahead of others, and water knows how to wait for the right moment. People who cultivate their minds should live like flowing water and learn a great deal from it.

MY MIND TREE

A TREE SHAKES when the wind blows, and it stands still after the wind passes. However, when the mind's tree hears a disturbing story, it stands still at first. Then, after the wind of disturbance passes, it shakes violently for days to come, thinking things like, "I should have said this," or "I should have said that."

What is the reason that the mind's tree shakes for many days after a single gust of wind? It is because it still has impurities. Unlike the mind's tree, all things in nature are calm after the wind passes.

Look at my mind's tree that violently shakes by itself in the moonlit night or on a bright sunny day. What would the stream that flows over there, or the rock next to it, or the birds in the sky, say?

KASHYAPA, WHAT IS THE MIND?

ONCE, THE BUDDHA SAID to Kashyapa: "What mind is the mind that is tainted by sexual desire, that shakes in anger, or that is blinded by ignorance? Is it the mind of the past, the present, or the future? If it is the mind of the past, it has already disappeared; if it is the mind of the future, it has not come yet; and if it is the mind of the present, it no longer remains.

"The mind is neither within, without, nor anywhere else. Because the mind has no form, it cannot be seen with the eyes, and it cannot be touched. The mind does not appear, it cannot be recognized, it cannot be named. No Tathagata has ever seen the mind. It cannot be seen now, and it probably will not be seen in the future. How does such a mind work?

"Because the mind is like an illusion, it appears in many different forms from the deluded discriminations.

"Because the mind is like the wind, it travels far and cannot be caught, and it does not show its form.

"Because the mind is like the flowing river, it passes without stopping.

"Because the mind is like the flame of a lamp, when it is lit by a cause, it lights up the environment.

"Because the mind is like lightning, it does not even remain for a moment and it ceases in a split second.

"Because the mind is like an empty space, it becomes dirty from unexpected smoke.

"Because the mind is like a monkey, it cannot stay still even for a moment and it constantly moves around.

"Because the mind is like an artist, it creates many different forms. The mind does not stay in one place. It generates many doubts at once. The mind goes alone; it is not merged with a second mind.

"Because the mind is like a king, it rules everything.

"Because the mind is like an enemy, it brings up all the suffering.

"Because the mind is like a house built with sand, it thinks impermanent things are permanent.

"Because the mind is like a gadfly, it thinks that what is dirty is clean.

"Because the mind is like a dream, it believes that what is not mine is mine.

"Because the mind is like an enemy, it always awaits and rejoices for weakness.

"As the mind is moved by self-righteousness or shaken by anger, sometimes it becomes arrogant, and sometimes it becomes dishonorable.

"Because the mind is like a thief, it steals all the good roots planted in the past.

"The mind likes beautiful color, like a moth that flies into a fire.

"The mind likes sound, like the sound of the drum on the battlefield.

"The mind likes the smell of decadence, just as a boar likes the smell of a rotten corpse.

"The mind likes taste, like a dog that salivates when looking at food.

"The mind likes the sensation of touch, like a fly stuck to an oily plate.

"Even if you exhaustively observe the mind like this, the true nature of the mind cannot be known. It cannot be found. The thing that cannot be attained does not exist in the future, in the present, or in the past.

"The thing that does not exist in the future, in the present, or in the past exists by transcending the future, the present, and the past.

"The thing that exists by transcending the three time periods is neither existent nor nonexistent.

"The thing that is neither existent nor nonexistent is never created.

"The thing that is never created does not have self nature.

"The thing that has no self nature does not arise.

"The thing that does not arise never ceases.

"The thing that never ceases never passes.

"If it does not pass, there is neither going nor coming. There is neither dying nor being born.

"The thing that has neither going, coming, dying, nor being born has no creation of cause and effect.

"The thing that has no creation of cause and effect has neither creation nor change. It is in the state of inaction. This is the innate nature of a saint.

"Just as empty space is equal to wherever it is, that innate nature is equal in everyone. That innate nature has no discrimination [between different beings], because in the end every being is from one essence.

"Because the innate nature that has departed from such discrimination of the body or the mind is peaceful, it follows the path to nirvana.

"Because that innate nature cannot be defiled by any suffering, it is pure.

"Because that innate nature has no attachment of 'I am doing something,' or the attachment of 'mine,' it is not mine.

"The mind's true nature is neither truthful nor untruthful. Ultimately, it is balanced, because it is not biased toward anything.

"That true nature is the most supreme truth. It transcends this world.

"Because that true nature is not originally created, it can never cease.

"Because that true nature always exists, it is eternal.

"Because that true nature is the most supreme nirvana, it is happiness.

"Because that true nature has been purified of all defilements, it is clear.

"Because that true nature has no ego when you look for it, it is egoless.

"That true nature is absolutely pure. Therefore, one should quest for the wisdom within and not drift outside oneself. Even if someone is angry at you, do not be angry in return. Even if you are getting beaten upon, do not beat upon the other person in return. Even if you are being criticized, do not criticize others in return. Even if you are being mocked, do not mock the other. Then look into your mind and see exactly who the focus of anger is, who is being beaten up, who is being criticized, who is being mocked.

"Spiritual seekers should thus collect their minds and should not be shaken in any situation."

—*From the Kashyapa chapter of the* Heap of Jewels Sutra

Nine

Wayfarer

———

BODHIDHARMA

BODHIDHARMA WAS A PRINCE from southern India. After entering the Buddhist order, he taught students in India and also went to China to propagate the Dharma.

Once, on his way to China from India, he found an enormous serpent lying dead on a narrow path. In the area of Assam, there are serpents that feed on elephants, and this was one of them. When this serpent's carcass starts to rot, it attracts poisonous insects with its odor and blocks traffic for three years. Neither Bodhidharma nor anyone else would have been able to travel on that road, and to clear away the carcass would have required a couple of hundred people. Such a group of people was not available at the time.

Carefully looking at the dead serpent, Bodhidharma found that it hadn't been dead for too long, so he shed his own body and let his mind enter the serpent's carcass in order to drive it away. After moving the thing for seven days with much effort, he returned to the place where he had left his body, but it was nowhere to be found. Instead, there was the body of a bald-headed man with a ruffian's face. It so happened that when a Taoist ascetic meditating in the caves at Kun Lun Mountain saw the neat-looking body lying there on the ground, he shed his own body and walked away wearing the better looking one.

Bodhidharma had already opened a Zen monastery in China and, at that time, was in the process of teaching students. If he didn't put on the ascetic's ugly body, he would have to wait for twenty years before he grew into a body with which he could teach his students again. So, he entered the ascetic's body and took its form.

When he came to China, his students did not recognize him at all. After spending a couple of months with Bodhidharma, one of the students said that he did not look like Bodhidharma, but that the way he used his mind—the way he carried himself—was like Bodhidharma.

Bodhidharma finally told them what had happened and was acknowledged by his students. This is the reason why portraits of Bodhidharma look the way they do today.

Bodhidharma's Dharma power, which enabled him to take off and put on his body, is indeed extraordinary. People who have not shed the desires of their flesh spend their whole lives as slaves to their own bodies, running errands for their bodies, while their minds' weeds grow up three feet high. We should be able to subdue and rule our bodies so that we can serve Buddha. Only when we can subdue and control our bodies are we freed from the desires of the flesh.

TWO MASTERS IN MYOHYANG MOUNTAIN

AT A SMALL HERMITAGE called Kŭmsŏndae on Myohyang Mountain, two monks, each just over sixty years old, were diligently practicing meditation. One day, one of the monks said that he wanted to go sightseeing in Seoul, so he took his knapsack and left for the city. After leaving the monastery, walking down in the direction of Anju and Pakch'ŏn, he saw a butcher working in a meat shop. He saw the butcher separating the meat from the bone, cleaning out the meat that was deep inside the bone. He thought to himself, "We should thoroughly clean out the discriminations in our minds like that. I suppose a spiritual seeker should also try to be a butcher."

That very night, when his thought had progressed that far, he shed his body and passed on to the next life. Since his Dharma had been awakened, any decision arising in his mind was realized immediately.

After a while, the wife of the butcher bore a baby. The baby was bright, and his behavior surpassed the ordinary. The old monk had been born as the butcher's baby. Since he was born with his wŏn to become a butcher, he was immersed in his work. Soon his family became wealthy from his diligence. In no time, he reached his nineteenth year.

Meanwhile, the monk who still resided on Myohyang Mountain was now over eighty years old, and he was nearing his time to change his body. For the first time, he searched with his mind's eye for his friend who had visited Seoul twenty years ago, and he saw him working as a butcher in the Pakch'ŏn area. The old monk, in order to return to the mountain in a different body, first needed to leave the hermitage in the charge of his friend. He looked at the young butcher with his wisdom-eye to see if his friend could return by himself. It seemed impossible for the young butcher to come back to the hermitage on his own, so the old monk went to Pakch'ŏn to bring back his friend.

When the old monk stood before the butcher's house and looked inside, he saw a well-built young man who looked about twenty years old, working hard. Even while the monk beat his wooden clacker, the young man did not look up but was intent on his work. After a while, the monk beat his wooden clacker again. The young butcher did not think that a venerable master would look for a man of such low birth as himself, and the young butcher pointed the knife at himself, to ask if the master was looking for him. The master nodded his head.

Suddenly, a question arose in the young butcher's mind: "What am I doing here?" And as soon as he thought to himself, "By what cause was I born in this household and doing this job? This is not the path I am supposed to follow," he took off his work apron and walked toward the monk.

Little children will follow their mothers home for dinner without any hesitation. As soon as the master nodded his head, saying, "Yes, I am looking for you," the young butcher forgot everything about his work. Determination arose in the young man's mind to follow the monk and return to his original path. I wonder if such determination came from the Dharma power of the master who wanted to take his friend back. Or perhaps, because the young butcher had been following the path toward Buddha for many of his past incarnations, he was suddenly awakened to his original path.

Just then, the young man's parents and siblings came out, having heard the sound of the wooden clacker. The young butcher looked at his family once. Then, without a word, he followed the monk who walked a couple of steps ahead of him. None of his family was able to stop him. The reason the butcher was born into that household was because he thought being a butcher might help his spiritual practice—not because he had any karmic tie to that household. Therefore, the moment he awakened a strong vow to renounce the world, no one could oppose his vow.

For many hours the master and the young man walked without saying a word to each other, not even "Where are you going?" or "Why are you following me?" Renouncing the secular life and seeking Buddha had been deeply ingrained in the young man for many lifetimes—it had almost become his habit. Soon, they were climbing past a hill and going up the valley. Even though it was the first time that the young man had been there, it seemed very familiar to him.

When they finally arrived at the monastery, everything seemed comforting to the young man. The temple ground, the mortar, the kitchen, and everything else was what the young man had seen before. Since he was hungry, he made himself a meal and then fell into a deep sleep. As he woke up in the morning, the ringing of the bell and the beating of the wooden clacker sounded so pleasant. After three days, his mind became calm and quiet, and then he was awakened to the ability to see his past lives.

At that moment, the young man yelled roughly at the eighty-year-old man, "Why were you so late in bringing me here?" Becoming a butcher had been to help him cultivate his mind, whether it actually helped him or not. Buddhist monks usually renounce the worldly life to look for their teachers and monastery at around age thirteen, and since the young man had wasted seven extra years, he complained to his friend.

The eighty-year-old monk said with a smile, "I was so busy with my practice and with looking into my mind that I didn't have time to think about you."

What a perfect and truthful attitude toward the practice of cultivating his mind! We usually attach our minds to money, fame, and material possessions. But this master was so intent on his practice, he did not even have time to pay attention to his friend's affairs.

The nineteen-year-old man and the eighty-year-old man were talking casually like friends, for there was no doubt that they had been friends in the young man's past life. The young man was probably diligent in his practice from then on, and his friend must have received a new body in which to come back to Kŭmsŏndae.

I was a monk at Kŭmgang Mountain for many of my past incarnations. Every time I received a new body, I looked for my teacher and studied under that teacher at Kŭmgang Mountain. I never forgot to renounce the world—enter the Buddhist order—at age thirteen.

Once Master Baek said, "Why didn't you renounce the worldly life when you were thirteen this time?" In fact, I did try to renounce the world around that age. One time, after I was scolded by my mother, I said to her, "Do you think this is my house? My true house is somewhere else," and I struggled to go north while I lived in P'ohang. But it was not easy. That period was my time to renounce the world.

In my youth, I was always looking for a teacher. I would go see anyone and everyone whom I thought to be wise and commendable, and my spiritual drive was strong. When I faced tough challenges, regardless of difficulty, I told myself, "How can I accomplish great things for society if I can't even handle this?" and always disciplined myself to overcome the challenges. Later my master told me that such drives—trying to find my teacher, to serve Buddha, and to become enlightened—were the awakening of my spiritual roots.

Spiritual seekers always look for the teachers or the monasteries of their past lives, for such is the vow of seekers. I couldn't go to Kŭmgang Mountain because the border with North Korea was blocking my way. But I found Sosa, where I had occasionally studied during the Silla period, and met my teacher again. He said to me then, "Now that you have come to this valley after so many years and have found me again, practice diligently." Even though I had never been to Sosa in this life, the hills and the rice paddies behind the monastery looked very familiar, as if I had seen them many times before.

Once my master told us that we had been devoting ourselves to the path over many incarnations. Because we had become so sick of training under the frame of monastic rules, however, in this incarnation we were cultivating our minds without shaving our heads and without wearing the robes of monks.

May all of us cut the weeds of ignorance in our minds again and again and renounce the world again and again, just as one shaves one's head, so that we can serve Buddha well, parwŏn!

MASTER HAKUIN

THERE WAS A JAPANESE ZEN MASTER named Hakuin who was revered as a living Buddha. The daughter of one of his followers became pregnant out of wedlock. Her father was furious and pressed hard to find out who the father was. "Whose bastard is it?" he asked her angrily.

Cornered, the daughter named an unthinkable person. "Master Hakuin," she answered. The father was baffled. Since it was the child of the master he revered, he could do nothing but forgive his daughter, and when a boy was born, he took it to the master.

Whenever his followers and townfolk asked the master whether it really was his child, he always said, "yes" with a smile. He gave love to the baby and raised him with great care. Consequently, his reputation was destroyed; some considered him a heretic rather than an enlightened master. His followers' visits also declined.

Master Hakuin, however, begged for alms and raised the baby with difficulty and gave not a single excuse. One day, the child's young parents came to see him. They bowed to him and shed tears of repentance, the mother saying, "Even though he is our child, I could not tell the truth to my father, for I felt that he would have killed me on the spot. I lied and told him that it was your baby. I saved my own life, but I have damaged your reputation so severely. How can I ever be forgiven for my sin?" The master simply handed over the child to them and calmly smiled without saying a word.

Had we been in his situation, would we have been able to smile like him? His is a truly enviable mind-set. A person who is freed from the notion of self has no such thing as an "I," so there is nothing to be embarrassed about.

Looking at this story from a different point of view, one might recognize the role that notions imprinted in one's past incarnations play in creating such mishaps. Through such a notion, or because of a similar karmic hindrance in a past incarnation, one could experience misfortune in this lifetime. Therefore, when you are wronged and no one listens to you despite your explanations, just surrendering your arising mind (such as your hurt feelings) and calmly accepting the situation may be the wisest thing to do.

Ten

The Path That We All

Tread Together

———

THREE VEHICLES

THERE ARE THREE TYPES of people who pursue spiritual practice: those who ride in the goat's vehicle, those who ride in the deer's vehicle, and those who ride in the white bull's vehicle.

Those who ride in the goat's vehicle follow the spiritual path because they do not like the sufferings of their bodies. They beg Buddha for their family's health, their economic well-being, and their happiness. These are the people who offer up one meal's worth of grocery money to Buddha and demand ten years' worth of living expenses.

Like merchants trying to make a profit, theirs is the mentality of doing business with Buddha. One must plant wealthy causes to be well off and plant happy causes to live happily. The people who ride in the goat's vehicle, however, only beg Buddha and forego planting the causes. But the goal of spiritual practice is to change one's poor mind into a wealthy one—to condition one's miserable mind into a happy one—because everything is accomplished with the mind.

Those who ride in the deer's vehicle have more wisdom than the people who ride the goat's vehicle. These people know that this universe is built from the results of planted causes. They try to achieve bright results by diligently planting bright causes. They conduct their personal relationships in that way. They put much care into their children's education from the beginning, they invest plenty in their businesses, and they keep up their health early in their lives. And with thorough mental preparation, they live while preparing for every situation in their lives. These people live their lives brightly and successfully.

Thirdly, there are those who ride in the white bull's vehicle. These people know that what happens in their minds reflects what happens in the universe, outside their minds. Therefore, they accept the phenomena of the universe into their minds to enlighten those phenomena. Since these people's realization is one with the entire universe, it is the great vehicle and the most supreme vehicle.

They view sentient beings' problems as their own and resolve those problems to benefit many beings. With this type of enlightened person's wŏn and capacity, wars and disasters can be prevented, and the people's minds can be calmed. Such is the path of the bodhisattvas, which lights up the realm of sentient beings. We should all ride in the white bull's vehicle to tread the path of the great vehicle.

WHEN ONE PURSUES THE PATH,
NINE GENERATIONS BENEFIT

JUST AS RADIO STATIONS send out radio waves, so the human mind sends out mind waves. The waves of the mind spread out in all directions of space. If a son who is far away in Seoul is sick or worried about something, his mother can sense such conditions through intuition or feel it through her dreams. This is the simultaneous transmission and reception of mind waves.

Similarly, one person's merit of opening his heart to the bright radiance—the merit of devoting himself to a spiritual practice—is passed on to nine generations in all directions: to one's ancestors, one's grandfather, one's great grandfather, and so on, up nine generations; to one's descendants, one's grandchildren, one's great grandchildren, and so on, down nine generations; to one's relatives, uncles, cousins, and so on. One receives and feels directly all the mind waves that go back and forth in all directions. Karmic ties are linked in this way, both vertically and horizontally, and involve thousands of people.

If you lack spiritual cultivation and are quick to anger, are unstable, or greedy, or judgmental of others' faults, then you will send out your level of mind wave to the thousands of people within the boundary of your nine generations. People who have karmic ties with you will receive such mind waves and will suffer from them.

However, if you have cultivated your mind well enough to use it at a high level, then you will send out bright and healthy waves. Thousands of people will feel joy through you. Also, if your practice is advanced enough that you can receive others' dark mind waves and surrender them to Buddha, you will liberate their inner sufferings, wash away their dark shades, and illuminate their minds.

Moreover, the number nine implies infinity, as in the expressions "ninefold palace," "ninety thousand li of distant sky," or "nine thousand worlds." In Buddhism, "nine generations" means a countless number of ancestors and people who have karmic ties with you. Therefore, nine generations could mean all the beings in the universe. When Shakyamuni Buddha attained Buddhahood, many people became enlightened. The entire human race is receiving one Buddha's grace forever.

There is a saying, "If a monk is produced in a family, he illuminates the household." If he is someone who has awakened the Dharma power, his household and his hometown will receive the benefit. If an enlightened person is born, the entire nation will receive the benefit. If one person attains the ability to see one's past lives, thousands of people will attain the ability to perceive their past lives. When one person becomes enlightened, the whole universe is illuminated.

Buddhadharma—Buddhism—is more than just what occurs in physical reality. The inner radiance, knowingly and unknowingly, illuminates the whole spiritual realm. May all become more enlightened day by day to serve Buddha well, parwŏn!

ABOUT GIVING

Start with your mind to practice the mentality of giving

VERY OFTEN, if people have worked their whole lives in public service or office jobs, they will pull out a cigarette only for themselves when they smoke. People who run businesses, however, frequently develop a giving mind regarding their cigarettes in order to close deals and get acquainted with clients. When the mind that has been conditioned for many years becomes firmly molded, actions follow naturally.

The giving mind is righteous and joyful. It is an alive mind. The begging mind, however, is a broken mind, a dead mind. Even with just a cup of coffee, the moment you decide to serve it to someone else, you feel secure and confident. At that moment, you are the master of all realms under heaven.

The giving mind cleanses that innate nature of pulling everything toward "me." Just as your arms bend toward you, people tend to pull every beneficial thing toward themselves. Such a trait is inevitable as long as people have egos.

When a poor relative or someone seeking charity visits us, we start putting up our guards first with our minds. It is the mind of not giving and of treating him or her coldheartedly. The mind is not material wealth. Even if we cannot provide him or her with the material wealth they seek, why can't we at least give with our minds? With material goods, you have to be in the right financial situation to be able to give, but mind is not the same way.

If your mind is always that of giving, it directly becomes merit.

Give of your material possessions to accumulate great merit

If you give with the expectation of being rewarded, that is a business transaction and not an act of giving. For the person doing the giving, the receiver's joy should be sufficient reward. If one can give equally to strangers and to animals as one does with friends and family, one will accumulate great merit.

When you lend money to someone, why not lend the money with the intention of just giving it away? If you did that, you would not be bound by the person who borrowed your money. If he paid you back, you would be as happy as if you had found free money. If the person did not pay you back, you would not suffer from it, and your mind would be free. However, if you lend with the expectation of being paid back, your mind will be concerned and anxious every time you experience financial difficulty. Such worries tie down your mind.

Donation of Dharma

Donation of Dharma means giving Buddha's teachings—such as the Diamond Sutra—to spread the method of cultivating one's mind or to share your experiences of spiritual practice with others.

The teacher gives his life to the student

The sun gives light to all life forms to help them grow. No matter how many life forms receive the sunlight, there is always enough. Like the sun, the Buddha gives out life to all sentient beings. The moment we turn to Buddha, we receive the luminous energy of Dharmakaya and gain new strength. By reading the sutras and by reciting Buddha's names or mantras, we receive strength from the Buddha.

A teacher gives the entire energy of his life—energy gained through his spiritual practice—to his students. Since students take away energy, he has to recharge his energy through spiritual practice. If, by reciting *Mirŭk Chon Yŏrae Pul,* you constantly surrender your thoughts to Buddha, your energy will be recharged and you will be able to give it out to those who need it.

Once, upon meeting a person who did not follow the spiritual path, my mind felt as if it were suffocating and in pain because I felt his painful mind. When your mind is calm, you can directly feel another's mind. While I was talking to him, a bright light suddenly came out of my chest and entered him. It left a big hole, and my body was depleted of all its strength. My mind felt smothered and uncomfortable, and my chest hurt as if it were burning. I had just witnessed the reality of how sentient beings take life energies from one other.

The bigger the luminosity a person enjoyed in his past life, the more advanced a practitioner he was, the more energy his mind tries to absorb in this life. If such a person does not cultivate his mind in this life, and his mind is full of karmic hindrances, his mind will try to absorb as much bright energy as he held in his former vessel. Therefore, when an advanced practitioner encounters such a nonpractitioner, it can be very painful for the practitioner. This is the same reason why sick people like healthy people, because the sick people receive the healthy energy. One has to practice surrendering continually to recharge one's energy quickly in order to give it to those in need.

Spiritual practitioners and enlightened masters give all their energies to their students. They give even their lives. To raise their students, they give without the discriminative notion of giving. Because such acts cannot be seen, ordinary people do not understand—the grace of one's teacher can only be understood at a high level of wisdom. My master once said that he was sacrificing his whole life to raise one student. The energy he gave out was so precious that one could not put a price on it.

We should always invoke this wŏn: "For every future incarnation, may we all meet enlightened masters and hear their teachings, practice their teachings, and brightly awaken to them, so that we may serve Buddha well, parwŏn!"

GIVING WITHOUT SEEKING REWARD

HAVING A HEALTHY MIND means having the generosity to give what is ours to others, though they may be fiercely attached to themselves and struggling with their lives. Our minds try to make everything ours, whether it is money, power, position, or someone else's mind. In trying to obtain these limited things, conflicts arise. The flame of conflict encourages even more "me," "mine," and "my victory."

In the mind that is freed from the "I," no attachment remains. That mind is an empty mind. Without the desire for others' possessions, the empty mind does not cause another person to put up his or her guard. The craving mind, however, is weighed down by such anxieties as "What if I cannot obtain it? What if I lose it?" because there is an attachment to the object that it seeks. In the healthy, giving mind, there may be some such worry as "What if the other person doesn't accept it?" but in the end, the giving mind is simply full of joy.

Once, when Master Baek was walking down a road with other spiritual practitioners, he saw a woman moaning in pain from drinking caustic soda. Seeing this, he told his students to take her back to the monastery and care for her. One of the posallims carried her back to Anyang-am, nursed her, and provided her with medicine.

Since this woman was in hellish pain, she showed no gratitude from the beginning. She couldn't overcome the physical pain, screaming many days and nights without sleeping, nor could she eat anything properly, because her gullet had melted from drinking the caustic soda. Furthermore, she didn't want to take even the expensive foreign medicine that the posallim had gotten for her. Thus, every time the posallim saw this woman, she began to think, "What am I doing with this total stranger here? Did I come here to serve Buddha or this hungry ghost?" and a feeling of reproach arose in the posallim's mind.

Seeing how the posallim felt, Master Baek said, "The healthy, giving mind does not quarrel over the right and wrong of the receiving person's weak and frail mind." When there is no ego, the giving mind asks nothing from the receiver. After one hundred days of devoted care and prayers, the woman was cured, and left the monastery with gratitude.

One day a year later, while attending Master Baek, the posallim passed by the Chinese embassy along with some other practitioners. The sick woman, whose name was Poksuni, was standing by the road with a baby on her back, apparently now the servant of some household. The posallim who had cared for Poksuni was glad to see her. She tried to go near her, calling out her name, but Poksuni ran away from her as if she were ashamed, either of the incident that had happened the year before or of her current status. When the posallim tried to follow her, Master Baek said, "Shouldn't you just be happy to see your successful mind—the result of your healthy, giving mind? Why do you try to follow that slab of flesh then?"

He was saying that saving the woman's life had been the success of the posallim's mind, for she planted merit through that virtuous act. So now, when she should have been grateful and satisfied with the results, why was she seeking recognition and credit for her deed? Once she heard this Dharma lecture, she was ashamed of being unmindful and of not surrendering at that instant and instead letting her mind leave her to follow that woman.

COMPASSION

WE RAISED MANY COWS at Sosa Monastery. Sometimes, they gave birth to stillborn calves. Whenever that happened, somehow the people from our town or the next town knew it right away and came to ask for the meat. Since our diet was purely vegetarian, and since the calf must have been born at our monastery due to a close karmic tie with us, we couldn't imagine eating the meat.

When we gave away the stillborn calf while wishing, "Feed those people with your flesh, and may you plant as much merit as you can," people took it gratefully. But sometimes no one would come to claim the meat. Usually people came within two hours of the birth to take the meat, but once in a while no one came even after a full day.

Our master said that if the calf had planted merit in its past incarnations, people would come to take the meat, and the calf would accumulate more merit. But if the calf had not planted any merit, people would not come, and there would be no one to help the calf plant any merit. He said that when a cow is killed in a slaughterhouse and becomes food for thousands of people, it plants the merit of feeding others with its own flesh. If it is reincarnated as a human, it becomes a wealthy person, with between two hundred and one thousand bags of rice a year. Master Baek meant that when you feed others with your own flesh, you accumulate great merit.

Once no one asked for the meat of one stillborn calf, and eventually the meat went bad. When the master saw that, he told us to bury the carcass and plant a fruit tree over it. If you feed ripened fruit that have used a calf as fertilizer to spiritual seekers, the calf gets to plant merit. However, it was during the summer, and I couldn't get a fruit tree, nor was there anyone around who knew about fruit trees, so I was at a loss. I had to at least plant a willow tree. After four years, the willow grew huge, fed by the nutrients of the calf's carcass.

That winter, we had other firewood, but I intentionally used the wood from the willow tree and heated the rooms of many spiritual seekers. As I was heating the rooms, I invoked a wŏn to Buddha, "By the merit of keeping these spiritual seekers warm, may this calf meet enlightened masters, listen to their teachings, and awaken to their teachings in every future incarnation, so that he may serve and accumulate great merit before Buddha, parwŏn!" Until I had done that, it had been a burden in my mind, but when I used the firewood and made the wŏn, I felt as if a weight had been lifted from my shoulders. I realized later that my master had given me the task to make me practice compassion.

After that incident, even when a monastery's cat died, we buried it with a thoughtful wŏn. We always found something that might accumulate merit for the past owner of its body.

MASTER WǑNHYO AND RACCOON CUBS

URING THE SILLA PERIOD, Master Tae An found some raccoon cubs that had lost their mother, and to save them he went to the town's public well to beg for some milk from the women. The women, deeply moved by the master's precious Dharma lecture, happily donated some milk.

Master Tae An carried the milk in a bowl and climbed over a steep hill until he finally reached the raccoon cave, where the young cubs were eagerly waiting for their food. Feeling pity for the cubs, he fed and raised them for many days with much compassion.

When the cubs had grown enough for their eyes to shine, Master Wǒnhyo came to visit him. Master Tae An asked Master Wǒnhyo to take care of the cubs for a few days, for he had some urgent business to attend to elsewhere.

Master Wǒnhyo raised them with great care, but two of them died. Wǒnhyo, who boasted that he was the foremost Buddhist master of Silla, could not face Tae An again. Master Wǒnhyo thought to himself that Master Tae An had been raising the cubs for fifteen days since they were still just tiny bits of flesh and blood, but because of his own thick karmic hindrances and lack of wisdom, he had caused their death. He deeply repented and took this as an opportunity to awaken his devotion again.

When Master Tae An returned, he consoled Wǒnhyo, "There was no way you could have held on to the those whose karmic ties were ceasing." A crow was cawing noisily in front of Wǒnhyo, who couldn't say anything. Then Master Tae An said, "Let's fill the crow's stomach and let the raccoons plant merit," and threw the dead raccoon cubs to the sky. The crow that was circling the area sensed his luck and snatched them away like lightning.

DHARMA-HITTING
TO ERADICATE KARMIC HINDRANCE

A<small>T SOSA</small>, we were sometimes short of hands while working on the farm, so we hired paid workers. Once, Master Baek found one urinating next to a well. Because people have led dark and ignorant lives for countless eons, they carry out such acts without even realizing what they are doing. If you urinate next to a well, the urine will likely seep into the water. When an enlightened person strikes that karmic hindrance—that ignorant act—the person who is struck by such Dharma-hitting does not repeat that act again in his or her next incarnation.

After scolding the worker, my teacher said, "Because I see it, I can't ignore it, and because I yell, people who don't know what is going on probably say that Master Baek is terrible."

Once I introduced one of my acquaintances to Master Baek, but my acquaintance's words did not make any logical sense. Suddenly, Master Baek shouted at him so loud it felt like the roof would fly off. I asked my teacher about it after my friend had left, and the master said, "He was the same way in his past life. He did not have any logic to what he was saying. Now that I have struck that karmic hindrance, however, he will be fine in his next life."

People's ignorant acts and thoughts come from karmic hindrances they have accumulated for countless eons. When a brilliant radiance without ego shines on an ignorant mind through Dharma-hitting, the dark mind is instantly freed from its karmic hindrance.

THE MISTAKE OF TEACHING OTHERS

AFTER MASTER ZHAO ZHOU's spiritual practice had matured, he traveled around China and taught many students.

Once he went to see his friend at a monastery in the Shan Dong area. His friend's twelve-year-old novice monk brought two and a half wheat cakes on a tray. Since Master Zhao Zhou was the guest, Master Zhao Zhou thought the young monk would serve him first, but the novice monk served a cake to his master first. Master Zhao Zhou thought that now the young monk would serve him the other one and that the young monk would take the half. But the young monk did not offer the cake to Master Zhao Zhou at all. Instead, he put the one-and-a-half rice cakes in front of himself and started eating.

Because Master Zhao Zhou liked to teach others, he said sarcastically to his friend, "My friend, you should teach that child well."

His friend answered, "I do not want to ruin him by trying to correct his wrongs."

At that moment, Master Zhao Zhou had a great awakening. He looked back at his past and thought to himself, "How many times have I taught people to go the wrong way." That novice monk accumulated great merit by awakening a master.

If a teacher molds his or her students with the intention of making Buddha happy, it is a radiant deed. But if he or she says, "*I* am molding them" and "*I* am teaching them," then it is the ego that is doing the teaching. The students feel uncomfortable, and they inherit the ignorance of their teachers. At such times, if the negative karmic hidrances of the teacher and the students clash with one another, the act of teaching cannot be a virtuous act. How often people bind and agonize others in the name of teaching!

A Buddha, who is perfect, can see the past, present, and future of his student with his wisdom-eye, and therefore can wisely lead the student according to the life the student has led. If you are not able to do that, you could lead a student in the wrong direction forever, or your student might end up feeling hostile toward you.

When someone asks you a question, answer him or her sincerely, and when you are not asked, do not force your teaching upon others. If you really want to teach, teach them after shedding yourself of the ego to teach, and then others will not be burdened by learning from you. For if you teach others only with your ego's desire to teach, you will be annoyed when others do not accept your lessons. Where there is annoyance, there cannot be the work of Buddha. At such a time, you should realize your limitation as a teacher and surrender that annoyance.

SAVING BEINGS IS BUDDHA'S JOB,
OUR JOB IS SERVING BUDDHA

MASTER BAEK LECTURED that the Buddha had cleansed all the eighty-four thousand discriminations from his mind, but there was still one discriminating mind left in him—the desire to deliver sentient beings. Once a Buddha, or fully enlightened person, surrenders even that discriminating mind, he or she remains as the radiance of the Dharmakaya, no longer receiving a physical body. That state is called *Tathagata,* and in such a state there is no desire to do anything. There is only responding to sentient beings.

Because Buddha is freed from "I"—because he has no ego—even when he leads sentient beings to salvation according to his vow, he stays bright and pure like the lotus that blossoms in muddy water. But when one who is not freed from the ego tries to deliver sentient beings, it is more problematic.

If you meet people and help them in order to serve Buddha, you impress Buddha's radiance in your mind and not the karmic hindrances of those people. However, if you step forward and say, "I will help and save others," then, in your mind, you fully imprint the people whom you've helped. Therefore, in either this or the next incarnation, you could easily become like those people—you could end up in the same situation. If, after helping people in need, you find you have imprinted their miseries in your mind and have become miserable yourself, it would be difficult to call your deeds bodhisattva activity.

Likewise, if you think that you helped someone, then because you are still attached to your help, you are bound to the other person through seeking a reward. Furthermore, in order to claim your reward, you might be born into that person's household. On the other hand, if you help others with the reverence of serving Buddha, you are freed from the karma of giving help and receiving a reward.

If you say to yourself, "I am helping you," your ego's poisonous energy burdens the other person, and your ego of helping makes the other person feel uncomfortable and ashamed. Do it instead in order to make Buddha happy and to serve Buddha. There is no ego in such a mind, and this will not hurt the other person's feelings. Leading sentient beings to salvation is Buddha's job. Our job is serving Buddha.

THE ENLIGHTENED BEING WALKS
ONE STEP AHEAD OF THE ORDINARY BEING

W E OFTEN FORCE OTHERS to do things that we haven't tried our-selves. We make them do things that are unreasonable. If you force others to do things that you cannot do, you imprint that action in your mind. As a result, in the future you will be forced by others to do an impossible job. How burdensome and painful your mind will be when that happens!

Likewise, you should not force others to do tasks that you were able to do previously but cannot do now. If you make others do a difficult job that you cannot handle in your present situation, you imprint sorrow in your mind.

Teachers should not present their students with subjects that are too difficult. A person who teaches others should be just one step ahead of his or her students. You have to lead them closely to give them the hope of being able to follow you. Also, in order to avoid showing too much of a gap between you and your students, you must cleanse yourself of your ego. Lead others by letting them learn one thing and realize one thing. Have them listen to one Dharma lecture and also practice it. Walk just one step ahead of them. Then, just as a puppy follows a piece of fish, they will follow you one step at a time, learning and practicing to gain all sorts of benefits. An enlightened being walks one step ahead of an ordinary being.

THE CHILDREN WHO PRACTICE SURRENDERING

TAEU, A FIRST GRADER in elementary school, had always heard his mother reading the sutra and had also heard Dharma lectures. He knew something about the practice of surrendering.

Because he was class president, he often had to go to the teachers' office. There were many teachers of whom he was afraid, and he felt timid, and sometimes, out of nervousness, he couldn't even speak to them. Sometimes he couldn't control his flustered mind—his face would turn completely red, and he would stutter, making little sense with his words. It was his job, however, and he couldn't avoid going, so it was always a problem for him.

One day, before he opened the door, he stopped himself because his heart was beating too fast. He turned aside and recited *Miruk Chon Yŏrae Pul* for about two minutes. Then his mind was calm, and he was able to go inside the office to take care of his business.

Ch'o-rong-i, a third grader, once spent two hours in the evening doing her homework. The next morning, when she was getting ready to go to school, she found that her five-year-old brother had scribbled all over her notebook with a yellow crayon. Ch'o-rong-i became so angry that she was about to hit him with her fist, when suddenly she had a flash of the Dharma lecture that said to surrender by reciting *Miruk Chon Yŏrae Pul*. She also remembered her mother saying that the child who surrenders well is the nicest child. So instead of hitting her brother with her fist, she hit the floor and cried, reciting *Miruk Chon Yŏrae Pul*.

Although they are only children, they are already putting the cultivation of their minds into practice. It is said that one who rules one's body is a sage and that one who rules one's mind is a saint. If we educate our children to rule their own minds, how bright and prosperous the future of this country will be!

Eleven

Reading the Diamond Sutra, Surrendering the Mind

———

THE DIAMOND SUTRA,
SHAKYAMUNI BUDDHA'S
SPIRITUAL HOUSEKEEPING

SHAKYAMUNI BUDDHA did not teach the Diamond Sutra to spiritual seekers at first, for it was too hard. Only after he had taught his students for forty years, when their practices had matured and the religious order was stable, did he teach the Diamond Sutra. Master Baek said that among the six hundred wisdom lectures the Diamond Sutra is the one that the Buddha wanted most to teach.

Buddha's lineage of wisdom was passed down by Mahakashyapa, the first patriarch of the Indian Buddhist order. Later, in the time of Bodhidharma, the twenty-eighth patriarch of the Indian Buddhist order and the first patriarch of the Chinese Chan (Zen) sect, the lineage of wisdom went over to China.

The shower of Dharma blossomed in China during the time of Master Hui Neng, the sixth patriarch, who was well versed in *prajna*, or wisdom. The sutra that Hui Neng read and practiced was the Diamond Sutra, the heart of Shakyamuni Buddha's doctrine. Master Hui Neng first awakened to his faith because of the Diamond Sutra. It was the sutra he received from the fifth patriarch Hong Ren. Even in the Zen sects that preach not using language to transmit the teaching, the Diamond Sutra is accepted as the main sutra and is read universally.

My master tried many different methods and became confident with the Diamond Sutra and the practice of surrendering. He once said that with this method one could achieve Buddhahood in a single lifetime.

The Diamond Sutra is the answer to the Venerable Subhuti's question, "If a good man or a good woman is determined to awaken the supreme enlightenment, how should he or she control and exert the mind?" Chapters 3, 4, and 5 directly answer Subhuti's question. In chapter 3, Buddha tells us to control our minds by turning all our useless thoughts, which cause us to be born as nine different sentient beings, into Buddhas: "All sentient beings will be lead to nirvana by my efforts." How then does one make Buddhas out of one's discriminating minds?

My master said that if you surrender every thought to Buddha, it will become a Buddha. He also said that the practice of surrendering is reverence arising from one's mind, not from someone's request.

In chapter 4, Buddha says to practice giving without regard to appearances of sight, sound, smell, touch, flavor, or any other quality. How do we practice the mind-set of giving without regard to appearances?

As long as one has an ego, one cannot detach oneself from appearances. On the other hand, if one purifies the ego, everything one does will be detached from appearances. As Master Baek said, "In order to purify your ego, whatever you do in your life, do it for Buddha. Instead of doing things for yourself, practice doing everything for Buddha." Make serving the Buddha the purpose of your life. By cleansing your ego this way, when your mentality of serving Buddha is mature, you can practice charity without regard to appearances. When you exert your mind in that way, free of attachment, your merit will be boundless, as incalculable as empty space.

In chapter 5, Buddha tells us to recognize that all of our ideas at our level are incorrect (for we still have an ego). He says that when we surrender all our inner discriminations to Buddha and see the universe with an empty mind, we will perceive the bright radiance of the universe, the Tathagata.

As you practice chapters 3, 4, and 5, gradually you will become proficient in the state of exerting your mind without attachment.

Diamond is the hardest of all minerals. Unchanging wisdom that does not break can be called *diamond prajna*. With this diamond prajna, the teaching that leads us from the shore of samsara to the shore of nirvana is the Prajnaparamita Diamond Sutra. After teaching many people for forty years, the Buddha named this teaching the Diamond Sutra, for he was confident that everyone could be enlightened with this method.

WHY ONE READS THE DIAMOND SUTRA

WHEN WE READ the Diamond Sutra, which is the Buddha's enlightened mind and illumination, we travel beyond time and space to three thousand years ago to Jeta Grove in India. We communicate with Buddha, whose mind and body were in their healthiest state. Since we open our hearts to Buddha's radiance by reading the sutra, karmic hindrances that have frozen solid in the corner of our minds melt away, just as ice melts under the hot rays of the sun, and wisdom arises within us.

Just as fungi in hard-to-reach places are cleansed by sunlight, cleansing and gradually illuminating one's mind with Buddha's radiance is the purpose of reading the Diamond Sutra. It is so hard to read the sutra at first because we have been practicing the dark mind for countless eons, and we shy away when we suddenly face its brightness.

Reading the Diamond Sutra itself is cultivating one's mind. To cultivate one's mind is to become similar to Tathagata Shakyamuni. It means reading the sutra over and over to emulate Shakyamuni Buddha's wisdom, character, and compassion and to plant merit just as the Buddha did.

When we read the Diamond Sutra, we eradicate the dark shadows of our minds, the shadows that cause misfortune, and we free ourselves from illnesses. If you diligently cleanse all of your bitter mind, your boggled mind, and your self-defeating mind, the difficulties in your life will be resolved, and your wishes will be realized. You will become aware [of the true nature of things], as your mind becomes clear and bright. Reading the Diamond Sutra is a way to practice reverence and serve Buddha.

HOW TO READ THE DIAMOND SUTRA

M ASTER BAEK SAID that when we read the Diamond Sutra, we should have the following attitude:

First, do not doubt that Shakyamuni Buddha, who was healthy both in his mind and his body, taught it to his students.

Second, believe that you are among his 1,250 students, listening to his words directly and trying to understand them.

Third, try to practice the things that you do understand.

Since it becomes too overwhelming if you set your practice periods too long, practice for about one hundred days at first.

The method of studying the Asian classics containing the words of saints and sages is different from studying European books. Even if you do not know anything about these Asian scriptures, just try reading them aloud at first. If you do this until you and the author become one, you will merge into his or her world.

This works for the Diamond Sutra as well. You should read it aloud over and over with reverence, as if you were sitting in front of Buddha listening to his lecture, until you become one with Shakyamuni Buddha. You should read it with the sound coming from your lower abdomen, one inch below the navel, in half-lotus position or kneeling.

TEN YEARS OF PRACTICE
AND NAMO AMITABHA BUDDHA

ACCORDING TO THE SCRIPTURES, we have to journey for ten trillion and eight thousand li to find the Western Pure Land, where Amitabha Buddha resides. The sixth patriarch, Master Hui Neng, explained this statement: "Ten trillion refers to the ten evils, which are karmic hindrances in our minds, and eight thousand li refers to the eight evil ways opposite to the eight perfections. Thus journeying for ten trillion and eight thousand li means we have to eradicate ten evils and eight errors." At such a time, we become Amitabha Buddha.

There is a saying, "Ten years of practice becomes Namo Amitabha Buddha." Once, a spiritual practitioner was practicing hard for ten years to meet Amitabha Buddha. After he was awakened, he found that he himself was Amitabha Buddha. This means that if we clear the ten evils and eight wicked ways we are Amitabha Buddha.

Master Naong left these verses:

Where resides Amitabha Buddha?
No matter how much I look,
No way to find him outside the mind.
By surrendering all the discriminations of the mind,
One attains liberation to empty the mind.
Then the mind illuminates,
Exuding purple radiance from the body.

Last year, the grand master of Songgwang-sa was quoted in a Buddhist newspaper. He said that, according to the scriptures, the period when Tathagata Maitreya will appear is due in five billion and sixty-seven hundred million years. This means that if one purifies and overcomes five gates of sensation, six gates of desire, and seven gates of consciousness, one can become Tathagata Maitreya.

TATHAGATA MAITREYA,
WHERE SHAKYAMUNI BUDDHA'S MIND IS

MASTER BAEK ONCE LECTURED about an incident that occurred three thousand years ago at Vulture Peak in India.

Having cultivated their minds well, five hundred of Shakyamuni Buddha's students were in their peaceful meditation, in a state of *samadhi,* free of the three poisons—greed, hatred, and ignorance. The Buddha walked toward them, radiating bright luminosity. The moment they saw the Buddha approach them, the Buddha's radiance was brilliantly reflected in the mirror of the five hundred empty minds. The scene was incredibly magnificent and beautiful.

Buddha spoke with much joy: "You are all so bright and radiant. Eventually, just like this, you will attain Buddhahood by purifying the mind."

But as soon as they heard Buddha's words, all of their illumination ceased at once and became dark again. They had thought to themselves, "Great, that must be it. Since I'm so radiant, it must be that I cultivate my mind so that I attain Buddhahood," and for a split second they directed their attention to "I." Their egos had risen to darken them again.

However, though everyone else had become dark, there was one person who was shining even more brightly than before, sharing his radiance with his surroundings. When Buddha looked into this person's mind, he saw one of even more reverence and gratitude. That person was thinking, "Lord Buddha, if it weren't for you, how would I ever have heard such a precious teaching about how to become enlightened through cultivating the mind?"

Then, Shakyamuni Buddha gave a confirmation to him, saying, "You will achieve Buddhahood, succeeding me. When that happens, you will be called Tathagata Maitreya." The one who received the confirmation asked Shakyamuni Buddha, "World-honored one, why do you just radiate your luminosity and not bestow it on sentient beings? I beg you to bestow your radiance upon all."

Having heard this, Shakyamuni Buddha praised him greatly, saying, "The Dharma that you expound will indeed be greater and greater!"

The one who received the confirmation was Ajita, a prince of Andaman. The country of Andaman is an island nation located between India and the Malay peninsula. To meet the Buddha, he crossed an ocean, sailed up the Ganges, and participated at the gathering at Vulture Peak. Before he started out, he had cut down a tropical bamboo tree much bigger than a man and used it as a boat to sail there.

The moment that Prince Ajita received the confirmation, he thought to himself, "How can I succeed to Buddha's lineage?" It took him twelve incarnations to cleanse that one discrimination that had arisen from such a heavy sense of responsibility. While cultivating his mind for twelve incarnations, it is said that he came to this world as many different saints.

WHY WE RECITE *MIRŬK CHON YŎRAE PUL*

SHAKYAMUNI BUDDHA praised Kwanseŭm Posal (Avalokiteshvara), saying that we would fulfill our wishes by reciting *Namu Kwanseŭm Posal*. For this reason, even though Shakyamuni Buddha is the basis of all, we forget about the Buddha. Instead, we attach our minds to the wish-fulfilling power of Kwanseŭm and claim that reciting *Namu Kwanseŭm Posal* is the best practice.

Bodhisattvas are the ten different representations of the Tathagata. Since we must direct our minds to Buddha, who is at the root of those representations, to become more enlightened, we have to find where Shakyamuni Buddha's mind has gone. Shakyamuni Buddha's mind has gone to the radiant place of *Mirŭk Chon Yŏrae Pul*—Tathagata Maitreya.

Reciting *Mirŭk Chon Yŏrae Pul* is the path to serve the principal Buddha, Tathagata Maitreya, who succeeded the spirit of Shakyamuni Buddha. One Buddha's period of delivering sentient beings is said to be three thousand years. At first a red lotus blossoms; after a thousand years, the white lotus blossoms; after two thousand years, the yellow lotus blossoms; and after three thousand years, it is said to become a blue lotus. When the blue lotus blossoms, a Buddha will appear in the world. There are supposedly lotus flowers that are nearing three thousand years old, alive since the time of Shakyamuni Buddha.

When I was a student, we used to calculate the Buddhist era to be around 2,990 years long. Back then, there was about a five-hundred-year difference between the northern Buddhist era and the southern Buddhist era. But at the World Buddhist Conference, led by Japan and southern Buddhist countries such as Thailand, they determined the Buddhist era to be about twenty-five hundred years long. Since then, we have been using this dating system.

Master Baek said, however, that it has been three thousand years since the time of the Buddha, and he gave clear examples. For instance, we can be sure that three thousand years have passed since the period of Shakyamuni Buddha by examining Master Hyech'o's travel record in Ceylon.

In the *Sutra of Maitreya's Rebirth Above, Maitreya's Rebirth Below, and Maitreya's Attainment of Buddhahood*, Shakyamuni Buddha describes the world in which Maitreya Buddha will appear. He says,

> At that time, the night will become as bright as the day [today we can play sports under bright electric lights]. Towns will be connected closely enough for a rooster to fly between them [such as apartments, and crowded city buildings], and glass will be paved on the roads [asphalt]. When we go to the bathroom, the ground will break open to clear away the excrement [modern bathrooms]. Bad fruits will be replaced by good and delicious ones. People will be richly clothed and life will be comfortable. Sexual relationships between men and women will have become promiscuous.

According to the scriptures, this is the period when the next Buddha will appear. May all sentient beings plant merit as bright as daylight to serve the coming Buddha well, parwŏn!

Twelve

The Repeated Cycle of
Birth and Death

———

THE MAN WHO RECEIVED
THE BODY OF A FOX

ONCE, WHEN MASTER BAI ZHANG of China finished a Dharma lecture, he noticed a man waiting to ask him a question.

"Is a great enlightened master affected by karmic causality?" he asked. Master Bai Zhang replied, "He is not bound by karmic causality."

"Now that I hear your sermon, my doubt is finally gone. Though I look like a man, I am really a fox right now. In a past incarnation I was a teacher of Dharma who gave Dharma lectures at this monastery. Someone once came and asked me, 'Is an enlightened master affected by karmic causality?' and I said, 'He does not fall into karmic causality.' I wasn't sure about my answer, however, and while I was doubting whether I gave the right answer or not, I was born as a fox for five hundred incarnations.

"Now that I've finally heard your Dharma lecture, I'll be liberated from the fox's body. Tomorrow, when you go to the mountain behind this monastery, you'll find the dead body of a fox. Please perform a funeral ceremony for it."

The next day, Master Bai Zhang went to the mountain behind the monastery. Sure enough, there was the dead body of a white fox, and the master conducted a funeral ceremony for it.

Some say that the man was born as a fox because he gave an incorrect answer, "He does not fall into causality," and that he was liberated from the karma of a fox by hearing the right answer, "He is not bound by karmic causality." But there is more to it than that.

The reason that the monk was born as a fox was because he had practiced a fox's state of mind when he first answered the question. The fox's mind is a doubting mind. After giving his uncertain answer, as a teacher of Dharma, he was unable to meet any enlightened master to confirm it. His mind was burdened with doubt, and because it carried this burden for many lifetimes, it received a fox's body. Receiving a fox's body for a fox's mind is the law of reincarnation. Only after meeting Master Bai Zhang, with the master's Dharma power, was he able to shed the fox's form.

Just as Master Wŏnhyo said that one thought arising is a birth and one thought ceasing is a death, so surrendering one notion is directly linked to solving the problem of birth and death.

THE MASTER WHO WAS BORN
A WATER BUFFALO

IN SOUTHERN CHINA, there was an enlightened master who had 1,250 students. It would have been great if all of his students were diligent in their practices and in their daily chores. However, many were lazy and they neither devoted themselves to spiritual practice nor planted merit. The master always thought to himself, "How wonderful it would be if only my students would work as hard as the water buffalo we have here at the monastery."

They raised the gray water buffalo to cultivate and till the soil and the rice paddies. Every time the master saw the water buffalo working hard, he thought very fondly of it and photographed the buffalo's image in his mind. Just as an image is impressed on film when you press the camera's shutter button, so the workings of the mind also deeply record both good and bad things. Even though he was advanced in his spiritual practice, the master did not surrender his fondness for the buffalo well.

Much later, it was time for the master to pass on to his next life. As the master was sitting in a lotus position, one of his students asked him,

"Master, where will you be going?"

As the master watched himself, the buffalo was ripe in his mind, and he saw that he would receive the buffalo's body. It was a baffling, shocking revelation for him. "How could such an accomplished master as myself get a cow's body?" But it was too late.

Even at that moment, had he surrendered that ripened mind of the water buffalo to Buddha, he could have liberated himself from it since his own mind had created the image. But he did not recognize this, and he answered his student without surrendering.

"I will receive the body of a water buffalo."

Thus, he had already made the decision. He did not know until then that he had photographed the water buffalo in his mind. Now that he had realized it, he could have surrendered that hardened impression. But an incident that you confirm is hard to revoke. Furthermore, spewing out the decision that is made within your mind is like declaring it to yourself and to the universe. Such an act is the reconfirmation and acceptance of the result.

Even though he made the decision for himself, if he had postponed his death for a couple of days and surrendered even the notion of his own confirmation, he could have been freed and purified. Or, he could have practiced surrendering at the moment of his death by reciting *Mirŭk Chon Yŏrae Pul.* This would have imprinted Buddha in his mind, allowing him to receive a human body and become enlightened. But perhaps he did not know how to do that.

Beings act like their previous incarnations for the first three years of their new lives. Although he was born as a water buffalo, when he saw his students, he often chased after them to teach them because they were neither diligent in their practice nor doing their work. Unfortunately, all that came out of his mouth was "Moo." The students, not realizing that it was their teacher, thought the buffalo was trying to hurt them, so they tied it to a pole. How frustrated and outraged he must have been!

One moonlit night, tied to a pole as a water buffalo, he was lamenting his miserable lot when Shakyamuni Buddha appeared with the bodhisattvas. Coming upon the master tethered there, the Buddha helped the master shed the buffalo's body.

Just as where the sun shines brighter, the shadow is darker, so too, the more you generate the causal mind—such as a buffalo's mind—in a radiant monastery, the more quickly you prepare your future body for a lower realm of birth.

When I was studying under Master Baek, our monastery was a radiant place. When I generated a causal mind at Sosa, my body would become unusually heavy and uncontrollable, and I would just be dragging it around. My mind was not bright. After being scolded by my teacher for being absentminded, I would intensely surrender such a causal mind. Sometimes surrendering it diligently for an hour was enough to free me from that future birth in a lower realm. After surrendering such a cause, my mind was refreshed, full of reverence, and my body felt light. If you don't surrender the animal body you are supposed to receive in the future, you will become like that master in China.

You imprint both extremely good and extremely bad things on your mind. If, however, there is no cause in your mind to perceive something as good or bad, your mind will be in a state of nondiscrimination. Therefore, you will not be strongly drawn to animals, and you will not generate the causal mind for an animal rebirth. Thus you should surrender every arising thought, good or bad.

KING CH'ŏLCHONG AND PAK YŏNG-HO

L ONG AGO, a wealthy man on his way from Seoul to a prayer retreat at Mount Odae saw a monk writing on a piece of fallen leaf. The man from Seoul asked the monk why he was writing on a piece of leaf, and the monk said that it was because he did not have any paper. So the man from Seoul promised that he would bring him a roll of paper when he returned to Odae the following spring.

In the old days, paper was valuable. Because copying sutras and practicing meditation were the only joys he had, the monk's mind was directed to the wealthy man from Seoul, always wondering, "When will he bring the paper?" The next year, the monk asked someone who came to a prayer retreat at Mount Odae about the wealthy man from Seoul. He said that the wealthy man was building a temple at Odae.

By the merit of building the temple at Odae Mountain, the rich man from Seoul became King Ch'ŏlchong in his next incarnation. By the karmic cause of directing his mind to the rich man—always thinking, "When will he bring the paper?"—the monk became King Ch'ŏlchong's son-in-law, Pak Yŏng-ho.

Pak Yŏng-ho always wore silk, since he was a king's son-in-law, but he always used gray lining for his clothing. Because he had been a Buddhist monk for many lifetimes, he had to wear gray colored clothing at least under his outfit to feel comfortable.

Just as the *Sutra of Causality* tells us in detail, one plants great merit by building a temple. One temple is the basis for liberating many sentient beings' ignorance, karmic hindrances, and negative karmic ties. It is a place where they deepen their good roots. Because temples allow for the creation of positive karmic causes with the Buddha and provide the opportunity to practice the Buddhadharma, building a temple, as in the case of King Ch'ŏlchong, creates exceedingly great merit.

As in the case of Pak Yŏng-ho, one is born near the person to whom the mind is directed during one's lifetime, for the mind is directed toward him or her again, even after the body is changed. By planting this cause in the mind, one becomes husband, wife, family, or friends.

PEOPLE SAY THAT good people frequently lead miserable lives, and the wicked lead fortunate lives. They blame heaven for being indifferent. However, causes for such situations have been planted in past incarnations.

A man lives his whole life with virtue and a clear conscience, harming no one. When it is his time to die, he laments. He is full of regrets, thinking that helping other people, volunteering for the town, and doing all the things that others did not want to do was just a burden for him and his family. As he is dying, he thinks, "Even if I have to cheat others or harm others, I have to be well off first! That's the most important thing in life!" And as he dies, lamenting his poverty, he imprints that last thought in his mind. When he is born into his next incarnation, he lives his whole life trying to be wealthy, without worrying about compassion or morality.

As a person dies, the single notion that he focuses on becomes the foundation of his next life's mind. Since this man planted merit by doing good deeds in his past life, and since all the people who were indebted to him will pay him back in this life, he becomes wealthy. However, unless he cleanses his mind of that last determination, he will bear that selfish intention throughout his whole life. People who do not know the whole story will say that only a wicked person can be wealthy.

On the other hand, there is a person who cares only for his wealth. He has no regard for morality or kindness. For his own gain, he even ignores his family. Such a person always realizes his mistakes at his last moment and sheds tears of repentance. Perhaps this is an innate morality or wisdom uniquely possessed by human beings. He regrets, "I have voraciously hoarded my wealth for my whole life, yet when I die I cannot take it with me." And he repents, "the most important thing in life is to be a good, kind person first."

Because he dies with this last thought of goodness in his mind, when he is reincarnated, he lives his whole life with good intentions. However, since he did not do any good deeds for others or plant merit in his past life, he is always poor. He will live his whole life being harassed by the people that he harmed in his past life.

KARMIC RETRIBUTION FOR TAKING A LIFE

IN CHINA, they have a long scythe called a *changnat*. Every time you swing it, you can cut an armful of grass. One summer day, a monk was cutting thick foliage and grass with such a scythe. On hearing the noise, a viper lifted up its head and was instantly decapitated. The monk felt a chill go down his spine, but it was too late. He recited Buddha's name and invoked prayers for the dead snake.

It is said that an animal that is killed by a human can easily receive a human body. Because the animal imprints the person who killed it at the last moment, it is reborn in the form of a human.

Twenty years later, the monk felt one day that his mind was unusually disturbed, so he meditated on it. He found that someone was coming to reclaim a debt. The viper that had died twenty years ago was coming to exact his revenge. A nineteen-year-old man then came to ask the monk to be his teacher. The monk wanted to refuse, but he agreed so that he could clear the karmic debt in that life.

Since they had only one room, they slept next to each other. The monk found out that for some time the young man had been sleeping with a knife at his waist, and that his eyes were becoming bloodshot. The young man was changing without even realizing it.

The monk made a dummy out of straw and hid it. Every time the young man went to sleep, the monk laid the straw dummy where he was supposed to sleep, next to the young man, and covered it with a blanket. The monk then continued his meditation at the other end of the room.

A few days after he had begun putting out the dummy, the young man suddenly woke up with his eyes half opened, still intoxicated with sleep. He felt for the blanket next to him, pulled out the knife and stabbed the dummy, then fell back to sleep. The monk was baffled.

All exchanges of karmic revenge between sentient beings transcend the bounds of morality and ethics. They paralyze human consciousness.

When the young man woke up the next morning, upon seeing the master the poison instantly disappeared from his bloodshot eyes.

Karma that has been intentionally accumulated will cause an intentional karmic retribution, and the karma that had been unintentionally accumulated will cause an unintentional karmic retribution. Death and injury in auto accidents are not coincidental or random, they are the result of causes planted in the past.

If you can live without killing anything, your future will not be painful. But if you have killed a living being, surrender the act of killing imprinted in your mind. It will lessen the karmic retribution. If you can surrender it completely, you can even free yourself from the negative karma.

KILLING SHOULD BE AVOIDED

PEOPLE DO NOT KNOW that when they kill an animal, the vengeance of the animal follows them around. In Korea, people used to slaughter a cow or a pig for wedding feasts or sixtieth birthdays. Since it causes misfortune, it is best not to buy meat that was killed specifically for you, or meat from an animal that you heard or watched being killed.

Even when you are sick, you should use medicine that does not involve killing an animal for medicinal purposes. People in Korea often boil goats, snapping turtles, snake-headed fish, and so on to eat them for their medicinal value. The animals that are supposed to become medicine are usually just receiving karmic retribution from their past lives. When it is time to exchange karmic debts with another, they might just get killed like that—in the name of medicine. Another sign that it is time for you to exchange karmic debts is an unusual craving for meat.

After living in Europe for eleven years, my sister brought the nicest leather jacket back for me to show her gratitude. She felt that she was able to live happily in Europe because I supported her education. It was the first gift I received from her.

When Master Baek looked at the jacket, he said that the vengeance of the cow was attached to it. He also said that since the vengeance of the cow is often attached to leather, leather products are not acceptable. So I said, "What if I sell this jacket, and print Diamond Sutras with the money to plant merit for the owner of this leather, the cow?" And he said, "Don't start any karmic tie with the cow. Just give it back to your sister so they can resolve it between themselves." I followed his instructions. To enlighten one person, he paid careful attention to everything that might become a harmful obstruction.

I used to have a sheepskin jacket, and Master Baek told me it also carried the vengeance of the animal. He said that when the original owner of the sheepskin jacket—the animal—receives a human body and sees the jacket, it will cause misfortune between him and the new owner. Since then, I have avoided leather products.

WHY WE CANNOT BUT SURRENDER THE MIND

WHEN I HAD JUST ENTERED Sosa Monastery, there was a person there who knew a lot about running the farm. He was very skinny and had a short temper. Once my master said to me, "Look at him. His snake's body has ripened, and it's shaking its head." With my master's wisdom-eye, such an image was directly reflected on his eyes, and when I looked closely at the man, it was just as my master said. I was so shocked that I thought my heart had stopped—he looked exactly like a snake shaking its head! I was troubled for the next few days. When I thought that anyone, including myself, could become like him through generating anger, I was worried sick. I knew I had to pursue the spiritual path, but following it was difficult.

Had I been ignorant, on the other hand, and not known that such a cause could create such a result, I could have lived my life without being burdened by it. I wondered why I had enough wisdom to know such a thing and to suffer from it.

Since it has conditioned a poisonous and vengeful mind, the snake holds its head erect and does not run away; rather, it chases after you with spite. Out of fear, I fiercely surrendered any anger that arose in me as if my life depended on it.

ABOUT THE REPEATED CYCLE
OF BIRTH AND DEATH

A LL SENTIENT BEINGS can be divided into nine categories. Depending on how each group of sentient beings uses their minds, they are born in different forms and are dragged into the fate of repeated birth. One's mind changes the style of one's life and one's environment.

Concerning those born from wombs, eggs, moisture, or by transformation

Let us look at four of the nine types of beings—those born from wombs, from eggs, from moisture, or by transformation:

Those born from wombs: If a being practices a dependent mind, it is born from a womb. For nine months, it depends on its mother's umbilical cord for its survival. After it emerges from the womb, it depends on its mother's nipple for about three years and is protected by the mother. Examples are mammals such as humans, dogs, cattle, and so on.

Those born from eggs: If a being practices an ungrateful mind, it receives the karmic result of being born from an egg. After receiving the nourishment from within its mother's body, it lives independently without regard for its mother. Examples are birds, chickens, ducks, and so on.

Those born from water: If a being practices a hiding mind, it receives a fish's body. Due to practicing a hiding mind while living on land, it can only live under water.

Those born by transformation: If a being practices a boasting mind when it is not qualified to do so, it receives a body born by transformation. For example, a fly is born from the transformation of a larva, and a mosquito is born from the transformation of a wiggler.

The case of different sentient beings

A dog's mind is that of scolding. A dog always barks—no other animal barks so noisily. Because a dog is made from a scolding mind, it barks with a scolding mind. The dog's mind is fit for a dog's body and not for a human body. When ninety-nine percent of your mind is ripe with a scolding mind, it completely becomes that of a dog and separates from the human body. Such separation of mind and body is called death.

A horse's mind is that of trying to get ahead of others. Because its wish is to win, it tries to outrun others, both on the race track and the battlefield.

A serpent's mind is one that tries to grasp a lot with a small body. Since the small body tries to grasp so much, it becomes long. The object it grasps could be money, fame, a man, a woman. In the old tales, there are stories about a big serpent protecting treasures in its coil. Such a thing is actually said to happen. It must result from the owner of the treasure constantly practicing attachment to it.

A venomous snake's mind is an angry mind. Since a snake is always angry, its body is swollen with poison.

A rat's mind is that of a thief. It is the mind that always looks for dark places and holes. It is neither confident nor righteous.

A cow's mind is that of being content with one's accomplishments. It is an ignorant mind that does not know what is going to happen in the future. Since it is satisfied with itself, its steps are always slow, and it is never in a hurry.

A fox's mind is a doubting and unbelieving mind.

A fish's mind is a hiding mind. It hides under the sea.

A pig's mind is one of being greedy for food.

And there are many other examples. Whether human or animal, a being receives a body according to how its mind is conditioned.

According to one notion

Land animals feel that their lives are always threatened. In order to avoid being eaten, they do their best to be alert and on guard. The reason why the urine of rabbits and deer smells so bad is because of their nervousness. Similarly, a cow always instinctively looks off into the distance to protect itself. Since they are so nervous all the time, hiding almost becomes their wish. When that wish deepens, according to the mental cause planted in the mind, the animal becomes a fish, for the hiding mind is that of a fish.

Once it lives under water, it feels confined. It wants to fly in the open. That mind causes it to become a bird in its next life. It always thinks flying would be great, but now that it has flown, it feels empty; it misses a warm, cozy place. So it becomes a fish again, and if it feels cramped again, it can be born on land.

All sentient beings receive their bodies according to the single mind they generate. Whether you receive an animal's body through practicing the animal's mind, through imprinting the animal in your mind, through the wŏn you have invoked, or because you have a karmic debt to a certain household, it all happens within a single mind.

As the scripture says, receiving a human body is as hard as dropping a needle from the sky to hit a mustard seed. Master Baek also said that receiving a human body after one dies is a rare occurrence and that receiving a human body three times in a row is very rare. If that happens, the person will be born as a sage who knows without learning.

If you were a child yesterday and you are forty already, the day after tomorrow you will be eighty. How much longer will you cling to your desires of flesh, money, and fame, and be dragged around by them, letting time fly by yet not cultivating your mind nor practicing reverence to Buddha? Until you are at the doorstep of death? Because we can only devote ourselves to the spiritual practice when we have received human bodies, each moment we are alive is so precious.

Master Baek said that by reading the Diamond Sutra every day and constantly surrendering all arising thoughts, anyone can receive a human body in his or her next incarnation, for you immediately free each animal mind with the radiance of Buddha at every moment. He said that not only will you receive a human body, but you will also free your past incarnation's karmic hindrances and karmic retributions. Your future will thereby become bright.

Shouldn't we, at least starting today, read the Diamond Sutra with devotion and surrender our discriminating minds diligently to receive human bodies for all the lifetimes to come? Shouldn't we eventually be freed from even our human bodies and escape the endless cycle of birth and death?

LIFE AS A WAYFARER

A WAYFARER WHO IS JOURNEYING to a distant place stops and rests in an empty house. He cleans the house thoroughly. He dries the mildewed things in the storage room and the rice that had become moldy under the shade. He washes and dries the sweat-soaked clothes. He waters the withered garden and the vegetables to give them new life. He cleans the dirty well until its water is clear. He fixes the fallen door papers, and repairs the damaged walls. He lives in harmony with his neighbors, and he concentrates on study, knowledge, and the cultivation of wisdom.

Then, early one morning, he goes on his way. The next house he runs into has plenty of food in storage, the vegetables are fresh in the garden, and the flowers in the flower bed are pretty, too. The walls are well built, all the clothes are clean, and a fresh stream flows by. His wisdom will be bright, his knowledge abundant, and he will be on good terms with his neighbors.

But at another empty house, another wayfarer, who is lazy, does not pick up the rice that has fallen on the floor. He lets the rats run around. He neither washes the smelly clothing nor fixes the broken doors and walls. He does not water the vegetables or flowers. Because he is heartless, he fights with others. He does not accumulate any knowledge or illuminate any wisdom. He just takes naps, and early one morning, he goes on his way.

The house he reaches after a long walk is so old that the walls have fallen. There is no rice, and the well is putrid. There aren't enough clothes, and the house is full of dust and garbage. The neighbors are all rough, and they fight constantly. He has no knowledge and no wisdom. He does not know how to do anything.

Everyone in the world receives the result of the causes they have planted. This is the life of repeated birth and death, samsara.

THE SOUND OF LAUGHTER

A WEDDING CEREMONY WAS HELD at a temple. During the solemn moment when the bride entered the Buddha hall, two guests in the crowd broke into laughter. It was Han Shan and Shi De. As if infected by the laughter, the guests, without even knowing why, started to chuckle. No one could hold it in. Eventually, they all broke into a roar of laughter, and the whole place became filled with people laughing out loud.

This was a once in a lifetime, all-important event for those who were holding the wedding. But since they were the hosts, they carried on with the ceremony, restraining their anger. When the time came for the beating of the drum, "boom, boom, boom," those two broke into laughter again. The guests also broke into laughter after they could no longer hold it in.

As soon as the wedding was over, the father of the groom rushed at Han Shan and Shi De in anger, as if to seize them by their throats. Han Shan and Shi De calmly smiled and explained why they were laughing. They had laughed the first time because the man's grandmother had been reincarnated as the bride and was about to become his daughter-in-law. They laughed the second time because his aunt had died and had become a cow and then died again a couple of years ago. Her leather had been used to make the drum that was used in the wedding, so they said they were laughing because the affairs of human life were so funny.

When seen by an enlightened eye, this world is a wide open field of repeated dreams and jokes. At the same time, for the ignorant, this world can be complete darkness without any sense of direction. The chain of karmic causality, however, goes forward with absolute accuracy.

Should we laugh, or should we cry?

Thirteen

At the Monastery

WHEN THE RAYS OF SPRING COME

THESE DAYS, our monastery is comfortably warm, filled with the essence of spring. The bright rays of the sun are mild, and the trees and the saplings are finding new strength.

Recently, we bought five eight-year-old sweet persimmon trees and five Chinese date trees. As I plant the sweet persimmon trees that have come all the way from Chinyŏng and the Chinese date trees from Taegu, my mind teems with joy. Thinking about the red persimmons and the Chinese dates that will be hanging between the tinted maple leaves, I am already excited. Because the sweet persimmons and the Chinese dates are exposed to the salty winds of the Eastern Sea, their fruit will become saltier and taste even better. Proudly standing upright among the other saplings, they have a fine look that suits the atmosphere of the monastery. I am surrendering even this beautiful scene.

When I was at Sosa, we also grew fruit trees, such as peach, plum, and pear. Fertilizing in the spring and personally pruning and covering the fruit with paper bags was such happy and meaningful work. Back then, I thought only about serving those fruits to my master. Now, as I plant the trees in my late forties, my only wish is to offer up the fruit to Buddha, who completely fills the universe. My mind is one of offering up everything to the delighted gaze of the Dharma-body Buddha, who remains full in the sky and always beams with a warm smile as I practice surrendering. It is the mind free from the discrimination of specially serving the fruits to my teacher.

At Sosa, I didn't get to plant the trees personally, for I had gone away to take care of other business, and when I returned, other practitioners had already planted them. I was disappointed. But now I harbor no such discriminating mind. I invoke a wŏn with all my heart for whoever plants and takes care of the trees and lend my hands to him or her. People often say, "A picture of a cake." This means that only when one is actually eating cake rather than seeing a picture of it will one be satisfied. Even with someone else's cake, however, if you offer it up to Buddha with your mind, how delighted will he be? If you see someone else eating, how happy will you be?

Some have suggested that we plant flowers at the monastery, too. But rather than growing something that is beautiful only, a preference for trees that bear fruit may be a more spiritual practice. I would like to plant more medlar fruit trees.

Today, I tended the monastery with the young practitioners. In order to pave a new farm road behind the aromatic trees, we raised an embankment and brought in dirt to widen the road. People drove their tractors across the monastery grounds, and dogs often entered the monastery, distracting the spiritual practitioners. We planted a fence of saplings around the monastery for a boundary. We put up a fence and gates to guard the minds of spiritual seekers.

In this monastery full of pure energy, devoting my life to making Buddha happy along with young spiritual seekers, who come with selfless ideals, and receiving warm spring rays with them is indeed the truest happiness. It is said that the spiritual practitioner's chest and the green forest in the early morning give out life energy. The reason why this monastery has become more radiant and peaceful is because of Buddha's white radiance and the power of the spiritual seekers' practice. A life without greed, a life of cleansing karmic hindrances, a life of illuminating wisdom, a life of planting merit before Buddha—this is the life of pure happiness.

As we sense the vitality in the scent of the earth, we work with the intention of raising life. Then we stroll in the pine forest behind the monastery. We wake up at three in the morning, when Bodhisattva Manjushri is said to give his Dharma lecture, to read the Diamond Sutra. We live in the radiance of Buddha. This life of peace and joy can only be due to the grace of Buddha.

Soon, when April comes, the chorus of frogs in the rice paddies around the monastery will sound like the recitation of *Mirŭk Chon Yŏrae Pul.* After finishing a bright and powerful practice in the evening, blissful energy arises in my lower abdomen, filling my whole body and mind with bliss. As I walk the serene monastery grounds, I feel that the Dharma-bliss of reciting *Mirŭk Chon Yŏrae Pul* over and over must be the greatest happiness. Since I have been residing in this monastery for quite a while, people tell me that there seems to be a thicker fragrance around me. I surrender even this fragrance as an offering to Buddha. Whatever it is, the moment you offer up something to Buddha is happiness.

Back when I was training at Sosa, I would look around as I walked out of the outer bathroom after finishing the evening practice. The warm and snug atmosphere of the valley, filled with the rays of the moon, was like that of Buddha's realm or the heaven of immortals. I would want to savor the beauty of the harmony between the white radiance and the moonlight, but dark energy circulates after 9:00 P.M. Since it might have harmed my practice, I would close the door and hurry back to my room.

These days, the worries that I had in my twenties about not attaining enlightenment have calmed down a lot. I surrender as I calmly watch the moonlight and the bright luminescence that spreads within the reaches of juniper trees.

THE MUD HOUSE

FOR SOME TIME NOW, practitioners at our monastery have been making a mud house. First, we dug up the mud from the mountain and mixed it with straw cut with the straw-cutter; then we compressed it in a wooden rack to make mud bricks. While they dried in the sun for about a month, we cared for them well, covering them when it rained.

We are building this mud house to use it as a drying room for *meju* (compressed blocks of bean paste that we use to make soy sauce). After we install the underfloor heating system and huge cauldrons, we'll boil the soy beans in the cauldrons using firewood, and the heat will dry the mejus. Having laid the concrete foundation, we laid about thirty centimeters of cement bricks. We are planning to build two twenty-eight-square-yard rooms. When the brick foundations have dried well, we will build up the mud bricks a couple of layers at a time.

The cement bricks that we used were also made by the practitioners two years ago. They seemed bored with nothing to do in the winter, so I ordered a brick-making machine. We built a greenhouse and made the bricks inside. At first we made some mistakes, but we made the bricks with care, all the while reciting *Mirŭk Chon Yŏrae Pul*. When the two rooms started to take shape, we made girders and rafters from the acacia tree that had been cut from the mountain near our monastery, and we fastened them with wire.

In the beginning, I didn't feel very comfortable, for we had started to build the house without any previous experience. Now that the house is taking shape, I'm beginning to feel more confident. I've built two houses before, but since most of the work was done by technicians, I didn't pay much attention. I've never built a mud house before. Since most of the spiritual practitioners here had just graduated from schools or gotten out of the army when they came, they didn't know much about building houses either.

Fortunately, there was one person who had some experience. After putting him in charge of building the mud house, I told him to intensely surrender any questions he had during the early morning and evening practice times in order to receive answers about how to build the house. The one in charge gradually proceeded with the work by realizing or seeing the answers to his questions after surrendering them. His questions included the problem of laying the mud bricks, of building the underfloor heating system, of placing the girders, of pulling out the rafters, and crossing the rafters and the girders. He said that sometimes he sought expert opinions or followed common sense, but surrendering by reciting *Mirŭk Chon Yŏrae Pul* had given him great wisdom. He has been studying here for about a year now. Building the house has been a good opportunity for him to plant merit, and it has also forced him to practice.

Because the practitioners at this place are learning to resolve their problems by surrendering each one to Buddha, I told them to take their work as their spiritual practice to cultivate their minds. This project allowed us to plant merit, to get some first-hand experience in building a house, and to practice surrendering thoughts that arise while we work. Eventually, we'll be able to build with our own hands the three-story great Buddha hall, where many will enlighten their human nature, and we can thereby achieve something that will fill our hearts with warmth. With this goal, all the practitioners' minds have been focused as one to build the mud house with reverence.

Master Baek has always said, "One should be capable and spirited enough to erect a pillar in the middle of a desert." What, if any, resources would be in the middle of a desolate desert with which to build a house and live? He means that we should be equipped with an aggressive creativity and the ability to make something from nothing.

On top of the rafters and girders, we placed the wooden boards in random order. Then we mixed chopped straw, mud, and water. The practitioners mixed them by stepping on them with their bare feet. The sound of their loud recitation, while mixing up the mud, resonated throughout the monastery. Then we carried the mixture to the top of the roof. The ones who carried the mud also did not stop reciting *Mirŭk Chon Yŏrae Pul.* After plastering the mud onto the wooden boards, we put the slates on top of them. It is a house made entirely of mud. A house I built in my past incarnation, by erecting a mud wall and personally cutting a tree from the mountain, must have been similar to this one.

Enlightening one's mind is like this. Whatever the task, even if you don't know how to do it or lack experience at first, if you keep learning and practicing, eventually it can be completed. Practice surrendering your deficient and incompetent states of mind. Proceed on your path by learning step by step and by practicing what you have learned. Having no notion of not knowing or of not being able to do something is the way to achieve the level of Buddha.

Lastly, we plastered the interior walls with mud, as we had done on the outside, so that there wouldn't be any wind blowing through the cracks. A fine looking house has been built, and because everyone feels good about themselves, my heart is filled with contentment.

We started a fire in the hearth, and the floors are beginning to warm up. When we hang mejus, the mud wall will absorb all of the moisture and dry it well. I'm already becoming excited, thinking that it will be a room in which to serve Buddha.

YOUNG SPIRITUAL SEEKER AND EARLY SPRING

THE FIRST DAY OF SPRING is only a few days away. The energy of the universe goes through a significant change during the change of seasons. There are two points where the biggest change of energy occurs. The first is the time when the long winter is over and spring is about to begin. The second point is when fall is about to change to winter, the time when paulownia leaves start to fall. The person whose mind is not disturbed around these points has awakened, unshakable spiritual strength.

Because they live depending on the earth, a slight tremor arises in the minds of young spiritual seekers as the first day of spring approaches. It must be that the unsurrendered emotions that were buried inside through the winter are now sprouting to the surface, just as the orchid prepares a new bud underground and sprouts up through the thick earth.

Since the old days, it has been said that, when spring comes, the heavy temple remains, but the light and careless monk departs. During this period, the minds of practitioners are very unstable compared to ordinary times. Their minds are full of wandering thoughts—thoughts about the world outside the monastery, thoughts about home. When that happens, usually their friends or families call or write to them. Since a novice practitioner sends out an unstable mind wave, the echo of that wave returns to give him or her a tempting answer, asking him or her to leave the monastery.

If one's mind were free of inner discriminations from the beginning, there would not be such contacts from the outside. But as a result of not being able to surrender that disturbed state of mind, a corresponding answer comes back from the people outside the monastery. If a spiritual practitioner can surrender his or her state of mind at that time, they can still free themselves from their discriminating minds. If the practitioner cannot surrender the unstable mind at that time, he or she might leave the monastery, enslaved by the unstable mind wave that he or she has created.

The mind wave that you create always returns to your heart like an echo. We cannot deny this obvious, ironclad rule. But those who strictly keep their practice times in the morning and evening, according to the precepts, do not easily become infected with spring fever. They all surrender well.

I've heard that cities are full of disturbances and accidents around the first day of spring. Automobile accidents increase in the streets, and people have more conflicts within their families or in the workplace because they cannot surrender their hatred of each other. Furthermore, since the first day of spring is before the lunar New Year's Day, the whole country is in tumult. Especially in times like these, we need people who cultivate their minds to calm their surroundings with the bright energy they generate from spiritual practice.

In the monastery, our minds are bright and clear in the morning. After three in the afternoon, people say that their minds are sad, somewhat depressed, and lonely. When a practitioner surrenders such a state of mind well at that time and goes on to do the evening practice, his or her mind will calm itself and become clearer.

We go to bed around 9:30 in the evening and wake up to begin our spiritual practice at 2:40 in the morning, when the radiant energy is brewing in the universe. Therefore, we are surrounded by the life energy, and in that refreshing energy, our karmic hindrances melt away as they arise.

While working during the day, whenever aversion to work or fatigue arises, we surrender such feelings at that very moment. Looking into our minds all day long and surrendering the arising thoughts and emotions, there isn't a moment when reciting *Mirŭk Chon Yŏrae Pul* stops. Here and there, all over the monastery, you can hear them reciting *Mirŭk Chon Yŏrae Pul*. Perhaps they have forgotten the fact that they are sitting on a toilet, but I sometimes hear people reciting Buddha's name in the bathrooms!

To completely solve the problem of repeated birth and death, these practitioners have been preparing a good environment in which to pursue the spiritual practice. Cultivating one's mind is indeed an important task. However, since there is no medicine that can cure one's innate nature, it is so difficult to change one's habitual mind.

When hidden karmic hindrances from many former lifetimes arise, some practitioners surrender continually for three hours in *changgwe* position in addition to our normal practice hours. To surrender the attachment that has risen in their minds, some people even sacrifice their sleep. Though I am sympathetic, their efforts to solve their problems by surrendering them one by one seem fierce.

Why have they, in their youth, rejected all other easy and comfortable ways to follow this path? Why are they working in the rough fields, exposed to cold winds, with no experience of farming? Why are they working in the mill, planting merit and living frugal lives? Their efforts to become enlightened, while forsaking money, fame, and pleasure, might not make sense to ordinary people. I suppose it is because they are the reincarnations of spiritual practitioners who have been cultivating the path for many incarnations.

Some twenty years ago, when I was practicing at Sosa, I often cut wood for fuel on the mountain in the winter by myself. In the desolate hills where all the leaves had fallen, cold gusts of wind would blow. The tips of my hands and feet would freeze, and become numb. On the days when even the sky was grimacing, it was especially scary, and I would recite *Mirŭk Chon Yŏrae Pul* to overcome my fear until my vocal cords were about to burst.

While going through pain and inner discord, there were so many days when I was sick of life at Sosa. When the pain was unbearable, I practiced surrendering and told myself that I hadn't been born in this life [trying to convince myself that this wasn't real]. Still, I spent my seven and a half years at Sosa worrying about not becoming enlightened in this life. To purify the attachment to one's body is painful. Why must we cultivate our minds through such hardships? I suppose it is the dilemma of everyone who tries to become enlightened.

As Master Baek said, the former Indian prime minister, Jawaharlal Nehru, is such a being that appears only once every five hundred years in this world, Gandhi is one who appears only once every thousand years, and Shakyamuni Buddha is one who appears only once every three thousand years. In order to become like Nehru, like Ghandi, and like Shakyamuni Buddha, even today, in this monastery, there are young spiritual seekers planting merit and illuminating their wisdom. Won't the future of the realm of sentient beings become brighter because of such people? It isn't coincidental that some people witness the radiance of Buddha in these young seekers, who reverently serve Buddha while forsaking the conveniences of modern civilization.

To solve the problem of eternal birth and death and to spread brightness to many people by serving Buddha, we should gradually cultivate our minds. Outside my room, where I am writing this book, many voices making offerings to Buddha are spreading high and wide into the rays of the afternoon sun.

Glossary

Sanskrit: (Skt); Korean: (Kor)

Amitabha Buddha. The Buddha who rules over Sukhavati, the Western Pure Land. In the Korean Buddhist tradition, practitioners who wish to be born in the Pure Land recite his praise, *Namo Amitabha Buddha.*

Ananda. One of Shakyamuni Buddha's first and foremost disciples. He was the cousin of the Buddha and became his personal attendant. He is known for his remarkable memory and is credited with being able to recite all of the Buddha's teachings.

Anathapindika's park. In life stories of Shakyamuni Buddha, the wealthy merchant Anathapindika figures as one of the Buddha's most generous patrons. He established a monastery at Jetavana Grove for the Buddha and his disciples. It was here that the early community of monks and nuns would spend the rainy season, and it was here that the Diamond Sutra was taught.

arhat (Skt). "Worthy one." A title of esteem and reverence for the senior disciples of the Buddha. More generally, a person who has completely purified their karmic hindrances and attained nirvana.

Ashoka. Ruler of the Maurya empire in northern India, who ruled from 272–236 B.C. He supported the spread of Buddhism throughout his empire.

Avalokiteshvara. One of the most important bodhisattvas in Mahayana Buddhism. He represents the compassionate activity of the Buddha. See also *Kwanseŭm Posal.*

Bai Zhang (720–814). Chinese Chan master of the Tang Dynasty.

bodhi (Skt). The wisdom of enlightened consciousness.

Bodhidharma (5th–6th centuries). The first patriarch of the Chinese Chan (Zen) Buddhist tradition. He achieved enlightenment after facing a wall in continuous seated meditation for nine years.

bodhisattva (Skt). An enlightened being who postpones his or her enlightenment in order to deliver sentient beings from samsara.

Buddha-eye. Enlightened vision that sees the past, present, future, and beyond of all things.

Cao Cao (2nd–3rd centuries). Military strongman who united North China near the end of the Han era through a series of bloody campaigns.

Chan. Chinese word for Zen.

changgwe (Kor). A kneeling posture where one keeps the hips and back straight.

Ch'ŏlchong. A king of the Yi Dynasty (1392–1910).

Dharma (Skt). Dharma with an upper case "D" refers to the teachings of Buddha. With a lower-case "d," dharma refers to any and all phenomena.

Dharma-hitting. An expedient way of purging the practitioner's karmic hindrance by means of hitting him or yelling at him. This can only be carried out by a truly enlightened master and must only be administered to a highly advanced disciple.

Dharmakaya (Skt). A Buddha's truth body: the essence of Buddha that has no physical existence but is represented by pure radiance or wisdom that completely fills the universe.

Dipankara Buddha. The first of twenty-four Buddhas who taught the Buddhist path prior to Shakyamuni Buddha. In the Chinese Buddhist tradition, he is considered one of the "three Buddhas of past, present, and future," together with Shakyamuni Buddha and Tathagata Maitreya.

Haein-sa. One of the three most famous Buddhist temples in Korea. This temple represents the Dharma of the Three Jewels.

Hakuin (1689–1769). One of the foremost Zen masters of Japan. He revitalized the Rinzai school of Japanese Buddhism by stressing the importance of sitting meditation and formalizing the teaching of koans—paradoxical riddles designed to lead students to an experience of enlightenment.

Han Shan (7th century). A famous Tang Dynasty poet who lived on Mount Han Shan (Cold Mountain) and is known for his unorthodox ways.

Han Yu (768–824). Chinese Confucian poet of the Tang Dynasty.

Hinayana (Skt). "Lesser Vehicle." Originally a derogatory term coined by Mahayana Buddhists to refer to some other schools of early Buddhism. Master Kim uses the term in a more positive way to describe a strict adherence to monastic guidelines.

Hyech'o. A monk of the Silla period who traveled to India to study.

Jetavana Grove (also known as *Jeta Grove*). See *Anathapindika's park.*

kant'amsim (Kor). A mental state that craves material things.

karma (Skt). Any kind of physical, vocal, or mental action that imprints in the mind and subsequently becomes a cause that gives rise to certain consequences in the future. Karmic actions can be positive or negative and either intentional or unintentional.

karmic hindrance. A negative action motivated by greed, anger, or ignorance.

karmic retribution. The results of karmic actions.

karmic tie. A bond that exists between people in this or future lives (or has existed in past lives) that develops from karmic actions.

Kashyapa. See *Mahakashyapa.*

Kwanseŭm Posal (Kor). "Bodhisattva Avalokiteshvara." Invoking Avalokiteshvara by reciting *Namu Kwanseŭm Posal* is a common Buddhist practice.

li. Chinese unit of measurement equalling about a third of a mile.

Mahayana (Skt). "Great Vehicle." A form of Buddhism that originated during the first centuries of the common era in India and subsequently spread throughout Asia. It stresses the importance of compassion and the innate potential for all beings to reach enlightenment.

Mahakashyapa. One of the ten great disciples of Shakyamuni Buddha. He was reknowned for his asceticism and moral discipline.

Manjushri. The bodhisattva who embodies the enlightened wisdom of Buddhahood.

mantra (Skt). Words of power that one chants during meditation or worship.

Maudgalyayana. One of Buddha's disciples who was well known for his magical abilities.

Mirŭk Chon Yŏrae Pul (Kor). "Tathagata Maitreya." Reciting the name of the future Buddha, Maitreya, is one of the principal spiritual practices advocated by Master Kim.

Naong (1320–1376). A renowned master of the Koryŏ Dynasty (937–1392).

nirvana (Skt). The ultimate state of enlightenement realized and subsequently taught by Shakyamuni Buddha.

Nongae. A patriotic Korean woman who sacrificed herself to kill the general of an invading Japanese force.

parwŏn (Kor). An invocation of a prayer, vow, or selfless wish.

pok (Kor). "Merit." The blessed fortune that stems from positive actions and is stored in one's mind that is the primary cause of one's future happiness.

posallim (Kor). Literally meaning "bodhisattva," in Korean this term is used to refer to any female lay follower.

Prajnaparamita (Skt). "The Perfection of Wisdom." A popular class of Mahayana Buddhist scriptures that includes the Diamond Sutra.

pratyeka buddha (Skt). A class of Hinayana practitioners who achieve Buddhahood without a teacher.

samadhi (Skt). A meditative state that is characterized by calm, stability, and the absence of distraction.

samsara (Skt). The cycle of birth, death, and rebirth characterized by suffering and discontent.

Sangha (Skt). The community of Buddhist practitioners. Also, the third of the Three Jewels.

Shakyamuni Buddha. "Sage of the Shakya clan." The historical Buddha; the Buddha of the present age.

Shariputra. One of Shakyamuni Buddha's disciples, reknowned for his wisdom.

Shi De (7th century). A Tang Dynasty poet and friend of Han Shan.

Shravasti. The region of India in which Anathapindika's park was located.

Siddhartha Gautama. The personal name of Shakyamuni Buddha.

Silla. An era of Korean history (57 B.C.–A.D. 935) in which the country was unified and Buddhism flourished.

Sin Saimdang. A woman of the Yi Dynasty who became a symbol of ideal motherhood in Korea.

Songgwang-sa. One of the three most famous Buddhist temples in Korea. This temple represents the Sangha of the Three Jewels.

storehouse consciousness. According to the Yogacara system of Buddhist philosophy, this is the last of eight types of consciousness that make up the psychology of an individual. Experiences of past karmic activity are imprinted upon it, until the karmic effects of such experiences manifest in future lives.

Subhuti. One of Shakyamuni Buddha's disciples. He is the principal interlocutor in the Diamond Sutra.

sutra (Skt). Any scripture that contains the teachings of Shakyamuni Buddha.

Tae An (571–644). A renowned master who lived during the Silla period

(57 B.C.–A.D. 935). He is known as Wŏnhyo's teacher.

Tai Dian. A Chan master of the Tang Dynasty.

t'amsim (Kor). Greed.

tarae (Kor). A type of fruit found in Korea that ripens in spring.

Tathagata (Skt). "Thus gone." One of the ten epithets of a Buddha.

Tathagata Maitreya. The title of the future Buddha who is to succeed Shakyamuni Buddha and deliver sentient beings from samsara. See also *Mirŭk Chon Yŏrae Pul.*

Three Jewels. Buddha, Dharma, and Sangha. The three foundations of Buddhist life and practice.

ŭmt'amsim (Kor). Sexual desire that craves the body of another being.

Upali. One of the ten great disciples of Shakyamuni Buddha. He was reknowned for his monastic discipline.

Vimalakirti. The central character in the *Vimalakirtinirdesha Sutra.* He is a lay householder who nontheless leads the life of a bodhisattva and is reknowned for his wisdom.

Vulture Peak. A mountain near the central Indian city of Rajagriha where the Buddha gave many teachings.

wŏn (Kor). A wish, prayer, or vow.

Wŏnhyo (617–686). A Korean Buddhist master who developed an indigenous form of Buddhism in Korea. Following his enlightenment on his way to China, he returned to Korea to write nearly one hundred commentaries on Mahayana sutras. He is reknowned for his iconoclastic lifestyle and has become an inspirational symbol for Buddhism in Korea as a whole.

Yashodara. The wife of Shakyamuni Buddha prior to his renunciation.

Zhao Zhou (778–897). Great Chan master of the Tang Dynasty.

ABOUT THE DIAMOND SUTRA
RECITATION GROUP

By following the examples of Dharma Master Jae Woong Kim, Gum-
GangKyungDokSongHweh (Diamond Sutra Recitation Group) is
devoted to the practice of cultivating and enlightening the mind. If you
have any questions, you may contact us at the addresses listed below.

NEW YORK :
46-39 158th St.
Flushing, NY 11358
Tel : (718) 539-9108, (718) 875-3576
diamondsutra.org

CALIFORNIA :
653 S. Mansfield Ave.
Los Angeles, CA 90036
Tel : (213) 933-6116, (213) 857-5696

ABOUT WISDOM PUBLICATIONS

Wisdom Publications, a not-for-profit publisher, is dedicated to making available authentic Buddhist works for the benefit of all. We publish translations of the sutras and tantras, commentaries and teachings of past and contemporary Buddhist masters, and original works by the world's leading Buddhist scholars. We publish our titles with the appreciation of Buddhism as a living philosophy and with the special commitment to preserve and transmit important works from all the major Buddhist traditions.

If you would like more information or a copy of our mail-order catalog, please contact us at:

WISDOM PUBLICATIONS
199 Elm Street
Somerville, Massachusetts 02144 USA
Telephone: (617) 776-7416 • Fax: (617) 776-7841
Email: info@wisdompubs.org
www.wisdompubs.org

THE WISDOM TRUST

As a not-for-profit publisher, Wisdom Publications is dedicated to the publication of fine Dharma books for the benefit of all sentient beings and dependent upon the kindness and generosity of sponsors in order to do so. If you would like to make a donation to Wisdom, please do so through our Somerville office. If you would like to sponsor the publication of a book, please write or e-mail us for more information.

Thank you.

Wisdom Publications is a non-profit, charitable 501(c)(3) organization and a part of the Foundation for the Preservation of the Mahayana Tradition (FPMT).